BIOSHOCK AND PHILOSOPHY

The Blackwell Philosophy and PopCulture Series
Series editor William Irwin

A spoonful of sugar helps the medicine go down, and a healthy helping of popular culture clears the cobwebs from Kant. Philosophy has had a public relations problem for a few centuries now. This series aims to change that, showing that philosophy is relevant to your life—and not just for answering the big questions like "To be or not to be?" but for answering the little questions: "To watch or not to watch *South Park*?" Thinking deeply about TV, movies, and music doesn't make you a "complete idiot." In fact it might make you a philosopher, someone who believes the unexamined life is not worth living and the unexamined cartoon is not worth watching.

BIOSHOCK AND PHILOSOPHY

IRRATIONAL GAME, RATIONAL BOOK

Edited by
Luke Cuddy

WILEY Blackwell

This edition first published 2015
© 2015 John Wiley & Sons, Inc.

Registered Office
John Wiley & Sons, Ltd, The Atrium, Southern Gate, Chichester, West Sussex, PO19 8SQ, UK

Editorial Offices
350 Main Street, Malden, MA 02148-5020, USA
9600 Garsington Road, Oxford, OX4 2DQ, UK
The Atrium, Southern Gate, Chichester, West Sussex, PO19 8SQ, UK

For details of our global editorial offices, for customer services, and for information about
how to apply for permission to reuse the copyright material in this book please see our website at
www.wiley.com/wiley-blackwell.

The right of Luke Cuddy to be identified as the author of the editorial material in this work has been
asserted in accordance with the UK Copyright, Designs and Patents Act 1988.

Library of Congress Cataloging-in-Publication Data applied for

9781118915868 P

A catalogue record for this book is available from the British Library.

Cover image: Texture of metal © Zeffss1 / iStock

Set in 10.5/13pt Sabon by SPi Global, Pondicherry, India

1   2015

Contents

Hacking into This Book (Introduction)

Luke Cuddy

When you see Rapture through the eyes of a Little Sister in *BioShock 2* for the first time, you see the evolving grandeur of the *Shock* games, an evolution that began with *System Shock* and has culminated in *BioShock Infinite*. As the Little Sister, you see an idealized reality, including a steep and long ascending staircase lined with teddy bears and some alphabet blocks, the surrounding white drapes lit brilliantly from above—all of this, of course, being interrupted by the occasional flashes of a much darker reality. Then there is Columbia, the breathtaking world of *Infinite*, a world that grows more mysterious as the gameplay grows more interactive.

It's not just the artistic complexity of the settings that makes the *BioShock* games an enthralling and immersive experience. The characters and storylines fascinate us as well. Center stage is Andrew Ryan, creator and ruler of Rapture. A male counterpart of Ayn Rand, Ryan was deeply dissatisfied with Soviet rule and left for America at a young age to seek something that the "parasites" could not corrupt. Even the mobs with less complicated backstories capture our attention: no player can forget the Motorized Patriots of Columbia, huge malevolent robots with wings that look like George Washington (no, this is not a Vigor-induced hallucination). Those are only a couple of examples. From the God complex of SHODAN to the Big Daddies to Elizabeth's tears to Comstock's self-proclaimed prophecy, the *Shock* games deliver compelling characters and absorbing plots.

The *BioShock* series pushes the genre of first-person shooters forward by expertly weaving role-playing elements into the game design. Ken Levine has rightly been hailed as a visionary, and the games have deservedly won numerous awards. Levine's attention to detail in developing worlds and weaving stories results in a series ripe for philosophical speculation. Players might wonder whether *BioShock* really does serve as a legitimate critique of Ayn Rand's philosophy, or whether Booker ever had free will, or whether humans in the real world will ever be able to shoot lightning out of their hands. These questions and more are explored in this volume alongside the theories of not solely Rand but Aristotle, de Beauvoir, Dewey, Leibniz, Marx, Plato, and others from the Hall of Philosophical Heroes. The answers go beyond mere musings on a message board.

You shall know the false philosopher, like the false prophet, by his mark: a claim to knowledge without justification. But you will find no false philosophers among the authors of this volume, each of whom is not only a philosophy expert but also a *BioShock* connoisseur. After reading this book, you will never look at *BioShock* in the same way again. Indeed, if this book leads you to read more philosophy, you will graduate from Little Sisterhood and you will no longer look at life the same way either. So, would you kindly turn the page and continue reading until the end of the book?

Part I

LEVEL 1 RESEARCH BONUS

INCREASED WISDOM CAPACITY

BioShock's Meta-Narrative

What *BioShock* Teaches the Gamer about Gaming

Collin Pointon

> The assassin has overcome my final defense, and now he's come to murder me. In the end what separates a man from a slave? Money? Power? No. A man chooses. A slave obeys... Was a man sent to kill? Or a slave?

Andrew Ryan's words from *BioShock* confront the main character, Jack, with the challenge of deciding whether he is a free "man" or a "slave." The challenge is especially difficult for Jack because he (spoiler alert, and more to come) was artificially created and psychologically conditioned to do whatever he is told—provided that the trigger phrase "would you kindly" accompanies the demand. Ryan's unforgettable speech and his last moments reveal the truth of Jack's identity for the first time. In the narrative of *BioShock*, this moment is earth-shattering.

Simultaneous with this game narrative is another narrative: the story of the player's interaction with the video game. The added narrative is what we'll call the "meta-narrative," because it encompasses the game narrative as well as the player's participation in it. What is fascinating is that the meta-narrative is also interrupted by the plot twist in Ryan's office. Ryan is as much addressing the player as he is Jack. In fact, the manipulation of Jack is symbolic of *BioShock*'s manipulation of player expectations. *BioShock* makes the player expect one game experience in order to falsify it not once, but twice. This roller coaster of meta-twists makes players philosophically

BioShock and Philosophy: Irrational Game, Rational Book, First Edition. Edited by Luke Cuddy.
© 2015 John Wiley & Sons, Inc. Published 2015 by John Wiley & Sons, Inc.

reflect on how games are created to affect them in strategic ways. Understanding how *BioShock* effectively manipulates players will take us through a variety of territories: cognitive science, philosophy of mind, philosophical hermeneutics, philosophy of video gaming, and philosophy of free will. It's all a testament to the brilliance of *BioShock* and a demonstration of how video games can teach us— even change us.

Mind Games

If you're like me, you just cannot get that image out of your head of Ryan screaming "Obey!" while Jack kills him. It still gives me chills. Indeed, all of the "*Shock*" games (*System Shock*, *System Shock 2*, *BioShock*, *BioShock 2*, and *BioShock Infinite*) have unforgettable moments. How video games like *BioShock* can affect us psychologically can be best understood through some recent ideas that scholars and philosophers have put forward.

The notion of the "extended mind," or "extended cognition," was popularized by the contemporary philosophers Andy Clark and David Chalmers.[1] This theory states that our cognition (or mind) includes not just the brain, but also the body and the surrounding environment. In one example, Chalmers makes the case that his iPhone is part of his mind because he relies on it to remind him of the important events, personal contacts, and other information that he has "offloaded" onto it.[2] He even suggests that if it were stolen, the thief would have perpetrated not only mere property robbery, but also significant mental harm–literally to Chalmers' mind! Whether or not you agree, it still stands that, according to extended cognition theory, *BioShock* can be a literal extension of your mind into a new environment—in this case, *BioShock*'s game world.

Undeniably, *BioShock* affects my mind, infusing it with philosophical ideas, and it affects my body, causing me to jump or making my skin crawl. We can tease apart these two effects hypothetically (the conceptual and the physical), but of course they are, practically speaking, always wrapped up together. Scholars have often remarked on the intensity of the cognitive and bodily responses that video games stimulate. On the physical side, Bernard Perron seems to connect extended cognition theory with video games when he writes of the "blurred distinction" between player and avatar. He even calls horror video games an "extended body genre."[3] However, gamers know that these designations are not specific to the horror genre alone. Video games as a whole are an extended body art form. For instance, sometimes when I'm gaming, I catch myself craning my neck, as if that physical act will somehow aid my avatar as I have him peer around a corner in the game world. That is proof of the extent of immersion (and *flow*) that video games achieve on a definite visceral and bodily level.

As a natural extension of my body, video games become a natural extension of my mind, too—that would have to be the case with extended cognition theory. As an example of an intellectual or conceptual stimulus within *BioShock*, consider the serious ethical dilemma surrounding the Little Sisters. The player can "save" the unnatural children or "harvest" them for extra ADAM. It seems like an easy choice for a utilitarian gamer, yet the act of harvesting looks (and sounds) violent enough to trigger self-loathing—enough to encourage many to refuse ever to "harvest." During the player's first chance to decide, Dr. Tenenbaum pleads: "Bitte, do not hurt her! Have you no heart?"

Empathy with digital characters or non-player characters (NPCs) has spectacular repercussions for philosophy, ethics, and cognitive science. Serious interest around player acts in video game worlds is strongly supported by Perron's observation that "mirror neurons" in our brains trigger responses not only when we perform an action, but also when we observe *another* performing that action. So, when a Splicer tries to harvest a Little Sister, and when Tenenbaum pleads with us, we are having cognitive reactions indistinguishable from those we would have if the same events took place in the "real world." Attacking Splicers triggers real fear, Little Sisters trigger real compassion, and these mean that video games can be spaces of real physical and conceptual judgments.

Rapture: How *BioShock* Hooks You

Since modern theories of mind explain why our brains are so vividly affected by video games, the next step for us is to examine how *BioShock* specifically stimulates us. Put another way: it's time to transition to what the game does, now that we know what our brains do (more or less).

BioShock grabs our attention; it hooks us into many unforgettable moments. Take for instance Ryan's speech mentioned earlier. Part of its memorability comes from the alluring presence and intense language of Andrew Ryan—whom the designers of *BioShock* modeled on characteristics of Ayn Rand, her philosophy, and her fictional characters.[4] Another part is the dynamics of the scene itself, like the player's loss of control over the avatar Jack, the dim lighting full of shadows, and the ominous background music.

Recall the first time Jack injects himself with a Plasmid. Suddenly, the player loses control of Jack and has to endure watching him stab himself in the wrist with a massive hypodermic needle. Jack then shouts in pain, his hands writhe in agony, and electricity arcs over and underneath his skin. Atlas says over the radio: "Steady now! Your genetic code is being rewritten—just hold on and everything will be fine!" Oh thanks, Atlas, how reassured I now feel, especially as Jack screams then tumbles off a balcony. The scene is horrifying on two levels: first, because of the unsettling sights, sounds, ominous music, and unease it triggers in the player about what will happen next; second, because of the player's inability to control or alter Jack's actions. The ability to control a character's actions is rare in other art forms like film, plays, and the fine arts. Player control (of one or more avatars, as well as viewpoints and camera angles) is a quality of video games that provides their designers an added opportunity for artistic choices. These choices might further singular or multiple ludic, thematic, aesthetic, narrative, or emotional goals. In the Plasmid episode from *BioShock*, the inability to control Jack intensifies the emotional horror of the scene, it bolsters the narrative of Rapture as a place of advanced technological innovation with disturbing consequences, and it explores the theme of the limitations of player autonomy.

Dan Pinchbeck calls the mechanisms in a game built to provoke particular player reactions "managed schemata."[5] For instance, forced camera angles in horror video games are managed schemata that incite tension, unease, and claustrophobia. The *Shock* games make great use of these elements. But managed schemata can be even more elaborate and quite subtle. Take William Gibbons' detailed account of the musical component of *BioShock*.[6] His analysis shows the impressive thought behind *BioShock*'s soundtrack, which includes providing an atmosphere of uneasiness, as well as moments of deep irony. Catchy, carefree, and upbeat music like Bobby Darin's "Beyond the

Sea" and Patti Page's "How Much Is That Doggie in the Window" are diegetic pieces in the video game that perform multiple levels of meaning and commentary. On one level, they merely enhance the feel of that time period. On another, they perform an ironic commentary on the narrative of the video game. (Whether Jack notes this irony is unclear, since he doesn't give us many clues to his thoughts and opinions, unlike Booker DeWitt in *BioShock Infinite*, who often talks to himself.) An informed player will pick up on the irony of the song lyrics as they relate to specific scenes in the dystopian underwater city. It is easy to see how these game-to-player cues formulate another kind of narrative, over and above the narrative of Jack's battle through Rapture: what I call the meta-narrative.

Gibbons analyzes the meta-narrative formed by *BioShock*'s music, noting that it relates, among other things, the irony of American post-war optimism, consumerism, and carelessness. Our focus, though, will be on *BioShock*'s meta-narrative as it pertains to the gamer and gaming, including the twist in Andrew Ryan's office and the utilization of the player's ability or inability to control her avatar: Jack. In order to understand this particular meta-narrative properly, though, managed schemata won't quite be enough. We'll need a philosophical fusion of horizons.

Horizons and Expectations in the Mid-Atlantic

When we say that we "understand" something, what exactly does that mean? This was the guiding question of Hans-Georg Gadamer's (1900–2002) philosophical life, and his books *Truth and Method* and *Philosophical Hermeneutics*.[7] Hermeneutics is the study of interpretation, so analyzing the way in which we interpret (or understand) written texts, art, or other human beings is a hermeneutic activity. The perspective in which the player begins *BioShock* might be called a certain *hermeneutic horizon*. A hermeneutic horizon consists of the wide variety of possibilities for interpreting something. Consequently, we are always working within evolving hermeneutic horizons as we go about in the world—and since each person has a unique set of life experiences, his or her hermeneutic horizon is slightly different from others'.

Beginning to play *BioShock* is not a matter of a player having an utterly blank slate of expectations. Rather, players have a hermeneutic horizon that consists of conscious and unconscious ideas of what the game is, how it works, what to do in it, how it will affect them, what they want out of it, and so on. Seemingly mundane presuppositions (Gadamer called them prejudices), like "one joystick is to move and the other is to look" and "this game will involve shooting," are ideas that make up the hermeneutic horizon. They can be so obvious that gamers are not even conscious of them. In fact, what is hard is to recall a time when they had to learn these presuppositions—something obvious when a gamer watches a non-gamer attempt to play a video game for the first time. Seriously, just ask your grandma to play *BioShock* sometime for a laugh (or is she actually a closet hardcore gamer?). Other presuppositions appear a little more complicated, like the presupposition of the avatar's freedom of choice.

As players progress through the video game, their hermeneutic horizon is shifting and altering in relation to the game—just like when you fumble around with a finicky controller and eventually realize that the batteries are dead. Tutorials, maps, and hints all aid in altering a player's hermeneutic horizon to fit the game space, helping the player understand how to interpret the game world properly so that maneuvering through it becomes second nature. A similar mechanic is at work in books like this one, where page numbers and chapters form a system for easily navigating and negotiating its content (well, that's the hope). Either way, tutorials or page numbers are signs to the audience concerning how to interpret something—they are hermeneutic indicators.

Gadamer often likened the dynamic of text and reader to a conversation between two people. In a conversation, brand new ideas can pop up that were never in the minds of either person individually. Their conversing is a *fusion of horizons* where a new space of possibilities suddenly comes into existence. This is also the case with video games. Players deeply engaged with interpreting *BioShock*, as they play it, find out more about the game and about themselves. It's an experience perfectly captured by Jerry Holkins, gamer and co-creator of the web comic *Penny Arcade*:

> I can't resist it. I always feel the strong compulsion to build upon whatever I enjoy, to understand it better. I can't listen to a song without harmonizing with it, and I can't play a game without imbuing it with sheaves upon sheaves of personally relevant contextual information.[8]

Gadamer would have been pleased to hear this. He might also have added that this process is always at work in us. When we drive a new car, for example, our actions are pre-structured by our past driving experiences. When we play a game, it is already couched in our personal expectations for it.

Just as rereading a book triggers brand new ideas and interpretations, even though the words remain the same, replaying games repays in diverse and unforeseeable ways. Perron seems to unwittingly invoke Gadamer at one point, writing that there is a "fusion" of player and game in "intentions, perceptions, and actions."[9] It is a pity, then, that Gadamer's hermeneutics is not referenced more in video game criticism, because the essence of hermeneutics is the important ambiguity between the interpreter and the interpreted—so too the player, the avatar, and the game world.

When *BioShock* begins, a certain narrative forms out of the expectations of the player (his or her hermeneutic horizon) and the operations of the game. It begins simply with the text "1960 Mid-Atlantic." The player's horizon shifts to accommodate this fact, like not being so surprised that Jack can smoke in the airplane (since it is 1960). What follows in *BioShock* is the development of a narrative where it is assumed that Jack is entering Rapture for the first time in his life. Later (spoiler alert), it is revealed that he is not.

The Meta-Narrative: Twisted Horizons

"Did that airplane crash, or was it hijacked? Forced down. Forced down by something less than a man. Something bred to sleepwalk through life..." When Andrew Ryan exposes Jack's real identity, Ryan is falsifying both the narrative of Jack coming to Rapture for the first time and the meta-narrative of the player operating a free agent as an avatar. The *first narrative* built around Jack is demolished and replaced with a second one: the narrative of a man bound by fate. In this case, though, rather than the traditional gods wielding divine powers as puppeteers—as in the uplifting tale of Oedipus or the cruise home of Odysseus—it is a con man using psychological techniques and advanced technology. Jack is supposed to be a tool, not a man, or, as Fontaine calls him, an animal bred to "bark like a cocker spaniel."

The narrative twist is obviously a trap sprung by *BioShock*. The game purposefully manipulates the player's hermeneutic horizon to fit the first narrative by only revealing very little information about Jack, and keeping Atlas's true identity concealed. Then, after the twist, there is a lot of information about Jack's real past and about Atlas.

Additionally, there is a *meta-narrative* twist. *BioShock* shatters the meta-narrative of the player enacting personal gameplay choices through the avatar. In a role-playing game (RPG) campaign like those in *BioShock*, *Halo*, or *Half Life*, players cannot customize their avatar. They must play as a specific character in the narrative of the game— but there remains some sense of freedom and personal choice, because the player is controlling a character who is free. Master Chief in the video game *Halo* seems to be a free agent, so the player does not feel cheated of autonomy. But *BioShock* is quite different, because the presupposition of the avatar's autonomy is purposefully and dramatically taken away.

Players react to *BioShock*'s double twist (narrative and meta-narrative) with the realization that their actions made no difference. They had to get Jack to Ryan's office, and kill Rapture's mastermind, because Jack is an unnaturally bred "slave." Players feel played and controlled themselves, and I think this is the product of the designers of *BioShock* replicating the emotional states of Jack in us. The presupposed meta-narrative is destroyed, and players are left with a new meta-narrative of being totally subservient. The manipulation that players feel is all the more powerful in relation to their presupposition of autonomy: the greater the assumption that Jack is like Master Chief, the more manipulated the player feels. As Peter Parrish and Tim McDonald write, Jack is conditioned to respond to other characters like the gamer is conditioned to respond to "Mission Control's" voice of instructions in so many other video games. But then, *BioShock* flips that all on its head.[10]

Personally, I didn't see the twist coming at all, and when it happened it caused me to reflect on what its repercussions were. Yes, I actually had to stop playing, and take a break—it was that intense for me. Gadamer said that there are always risks in any case of a fusion of horizons. One of these risks is having a completely unforeseen experience, or the risk of being changed yourself by the horizon of the "other"—whether the other is a person, a book, a work of art, or a video game. Is this not precisely what happens at the twist of *BioShock*?

The player plods through the game with a certain hermeneutic horizon that the game maintains up until the twist. Then, it pulls the rug out from under that horizon. The game invalidates it.

When successful, BioShock's twist sends players reeling. They are left holding fragments of their naive horizon, and broken concepts of what kind of game BioShock was expected to be. When replaying BioShock, one can't help but pick up on all of the hints of the twist throughout the game—like every appearance of the phrase "would you kindly," and Jack's ability to use the "genetic key." We can't put ourselves back in the mindset we had before the twist, though, at least not without awareness of our naivety and maybe a twinge of nostalgia. If players really let BioShock affect them, it will push them to self-critique and self-reflection (the kind Gadamer speaks of in "On the Scope and Function of Hermeneutical Reflection").[11]

Gaming Freedom: Choosing or Obeying?

The self-reflection that BioShock produces leads to a realization of the limitations of RPGs. The player has very little freedom of choice in BioShock, because if the player were to choose not to do as Atlas asks of Jack, then no more of BioShock's narrative could be experienced. You can't just waltz over to another part of Rapture any time you like, or play through the game's levels in any sequence you want. As gamers, we by and large have to do what NPCs ask of us in RPGs. Their "request" is no real request at all. It is a demand, which repays in plot and level progression (along with whatever other payment system exists in the game, be it ADAM, coins, or high scores).

We have the choice of what weapons or Plasmids to use, but the quest and its completion are set—just like Jack's fate to kill Ryan, or (spoiler alert) Booker's fate to become Comstock in BioShock Infinite. The BioShock series features much fatalism, and since the first BioShock also explicitly offers the philosophy of Andrew Ryan—with his stance that not to have a choice means being a slave—then gamers must be slaves. How could it be otherwise? We might choose this or that play style, but we are left obeying NPCs. Fortunately, all of this is merely the narrative and meta-narrative from the plot twist of BioShock and not quite its end (there is a similar progression in Infinite). In the final moments, these games change.

BioShock and *BioShock 2,* unlike *BioShock Infinite,* have alternative endings. In *BioShock,* the alternative endings provide a third hermeneutic horizon to understand the game. In case I lost you (I don't blame you), the first horizon (beginning with "1960 Mid-Atlantic") generates the assumption that *BioShock* is like other RPGs, but that is demolished by the plot twist and replaced with a second horizon about fatalism. That (second) horizon is then replaced with a new horizon about choice, free will, and freedom: the third hermeneutic horizon.

At first it seems that the Little Sisters are devilish additions because they bolster the illusion of player choice and autonomy in the game. However, at *BioShock*'s conclusion they have a significant impact on the narrative's ending, and so too the meta-narrative's ending. If it had one narrative ending, *BioShock*'s meta-narrative would remain within the second horizon and be philosophically about fatalism and the player's role as a "slave." Instead, the multiple endings provide a meta-narrative about the possibility of real choice.

Players cannot choose anything whatsoever they want in *BioShock,* but there are a few alternative endings to choose among. Harvesting all the Little Sisters (spoiler alert) results in an evil ending, harvesting a few gives a more neutral ending, and saving all of them leads to a happy ending. Jack fights against his psychological conditioning and succeeds in overcoming its control. That victory symbolizes players' freedom to see fitting endings in relation to their choices about what to do with the Little Sisters. Jack had to kill Ryan, but he could live as a "man" by fighting Fontaine. Players too must follow the orders of many NPCs, but harvesting and saving are real free choices. In the end, *BioShock* offers a critique of most other RPGs that present a "free" agent as an avatar. If players can't alter the game's narrative, then every choice leads ultimately to the same ending—in this case players can only "obey!" or give up on finishing the video game. But when players can actually alter the narrative, they operate a real free agent and there isn't an underlying illusion of autonomy.

In the end, *BioShock* seeks to be understood by Ryan's philosophical stance that "a man chooses, a slave obeys." With the first horizon, it masquerades as a game of choice, making the player into a "man"— the kind of meta-narrative typical of other RPGs. The second horizon reveals the fault of the first meta-narrative, because the player is a mere "slave" if his or her choices don't result in any different consequences. The third horizon finally makes room for the player as a "man" again, due to alternative narratives involving choices concerning the Little Sisters. This whole philosophical path of discovery could never extend to the player in a standard video game campaign where the narrative is unchanging. Indeed, how can we look at RPGs the same after playing *BioShock*?

Shock gamers are always on the lookout for the way games typically appear free but are in fact linear sequences of levels, plot development, exposition, scenes, and possibilities—making them ride over the same rails again, and again, like a roller coaster. That doesn't mean they aren't fun. It's still a roller coaster! But Gadamer would say that we can't go back into our old hermeneutic horizon about traditional video games. Linear games will still feel linear. A real experience means we're changed forever because that old horizon, or state of consciousness, will remain naive to us. It reminds me of Sander Cohen's curse: "I want to take the ears off, but I can't!"

It would take a sandbox game like *Fallout 3* or *The Elder Scrolls V: Skyrim* to let gamers act out the kind of complete freedom they might desire in a game: to do whatever they choose. But that has its own limitations. For instance, in sandbox games the player's experiences aren't as well managed. *BioShock* carefully introduces characters like the Big Daddy, Little Sisters, and Splicers. We see them, and learn about them, before we have to fight them. That builds tension, expectation, and it gives a dramatic conclusion in a way difficult for sandbox games to replicate. *BioShock* plants itself in a kind of middle ground: enough limitation of player choice to create a consistent meta-narrative, but enough freedom to sustain a sense of player autonomy. Which, then, is more satisfying? Carefully designed encounters within a flowing narrative, or a sequence of events that are self-guided?

Well, would you kindly not look at me for the answer? Just don't forget some existential advice from Ryan: "We all make choices, but in the end our choices make us."

Notes

1. Andy Clark and David J. Chalmers, "The Extended Mind," http://consc. net/papers/extended.html. For a critique, and more, on "extended cognition theory," see Frederick Adams and Kenneth Aizawa, *The Bounds of Cognition* (Chichester: Wiley-Blackwell, 2008).

2. David Chalmers, "Is Your Phone Part of Your Mind?" presentation at TEDxSydney, http://www.youtube.com/watch?v=ksasPjrYFTg.

3. Bernard Perron, "The Survival Horror: The Extended Body Genre," in *Horror Video Games: Essays on the Fusion of Fear and Play*, ed. Bernard Perron (Jefferson, NC: McFarland & Company, 2009). Kindle edition.

4. "Rationalizing Rapture with *BioShock*'s Ken Levine," *Gamespy*, June 25, 2007, http://pc.gamespy.com/pc/bioshock/799319p3.html.

5. Dan Pinchbeck, "Shock, Horror: First-Person Gaming, Horror, and the Art of Ludic Manipulation," in *Horror Video Games: Essays on the Fusion of Fear and Play*, ed. Bernard Perron (Jefferson, NC: McFarland & Company, 2009). Kindle edition.

6. William Gibbons, "Wrap Your Troubles in Dreams: Popular Music, Narrative, and Dystopia in BioShock," *Game Studies* 11(2011), http://gamestudies.org/1103/articles/gibbons.

7. Hans-Georg Gadamer, *Truth and Method*, 2nd. ed., trans. Joel Weinsheimer and Donald G. Marshall (New York: Continuum International Publishing Group, 2006). Kindle edition. Hans-Georg Gadamer, *Philosophical Hermeneutics*, trans. David E. Linge (Berkeley: University of California Press, 1976).

8. Jerry Holkins, "Rigorous Scholarship," *Penny Arcade*, January 11, 2008, http://www.penny-arcade.com/comic/2008/01/11.

9. Perron, "The Survival Horror."

10. Peter Parrish, "The Bird, or the Cage: What *BioShock Infinite* Says about Choice and Fatalism." IncGamers. April 8, 2013, http://www.incgamers.com/2013/04/the-bird-or-the-cage-what-BioShock-infinite-says-about-choice-and-fatalism.

11. Hans-Georg Gadamer, "On the Scope and Function of Hermeneutical Reflection," in *Philosophical Hermeneutics*, 18–43.

The Value of Art in *BioShock*
Ayn Rand, Emotion, and Choice

Jason Rose

BioShock made a big splash not only for the depth of its subject matter, but also for the way it utilized its video game medium to present its big ideas in a uniquely engaging way. The game weaves many themes into its complicated narrative, complete with shifting identities, science fiction superpowers, and survival-horror overtones. As a result, it can be difficult to pick out what Ayn Rand's (1905–82) philosophy of Objectivism says and what *BioShock* offers in response. Rand, who developed her philosophy of "enlightened self-interest" in novels and essays written in the 1940s and 1950s, was heavily influenced by events in her childhood—the Russian Revolution took her family's business and left them starving. Before becoming a United States citizen in 1931, Rand was so impressed with the skyline of Manhattan when she saw it in 1926 that she cried what she called "tears of splendor."[1] It is no accident that Andrew Ryan's biography reads as almost identical to Rand's.

It is clear that *BioShock* wants to be taken as a spiritual sequel to Rand's philosophical novel *Atlas Shrugged*, revealing a possible fate for John Galt's mysterious hidden utopia, sought after for much of the novel but never fully revealed, as the book ends just before Galt discloses his society and its plans for the world.[2] On the one hand, it seems rather unfair for *BioShock* to bill itself as a reimagining and a critique of Rand's works by making Andrew Ryan's version of Galt's utopian Atlantis a place of dystopian horror. Are we to think less of

BioShock and Philosophy: Irrational Game, Rational Book, First Edition. Edited by Luke Cuddy.
© 2015 John Wiley & Sons, Inc. Published 2015 by John Wiley & Sons, Inc.

Rand simply because *BioShock* depicts a possible result of her ideology as very, very undesirable? In fact, I don't think *BioShock* is guilty of this cheap rhetorical trick, but to explain why, I must first clarify what Ayn Rand herself has to say about art, emotions, and ethics. Then, we can see how *BioShock* makes its philosophical points on these topics through its narrative and gameplay. Finally, this will put us in a better position to judge whether *BioShock* creator Ken Levine is fair in his treatment of Rand.

Ayn Rand on Art, Ethics, and Choice

If you have played and enjoyed *BioShock*, you probably know Rand's Objectivist bottom line: society benefits most if everyone is free to act in their own enlightened self-interest, with "enlightened" here referring to fair play and mutual respect for one's peers. Andrew Ryan refers to "The Great Chain of Industry" as a wonderful metaphor for this outlook on enlightenment-through-capitalism. Frank Fontaine, on the other hand, is an excellent example of the kind of unenlightened selfishness that Rand would never advocate. Starting Fontaine Futuristics to capitalize on the discovery of ADAM on the ocean floor was ambitious, perhaps, but not villainous. Pretending to be a revolutionary figure named Atlas and leading Rapture into a civil war so that he can monopolize the ADAM and conquer the surface world certainly *was* villainous, and no Objectivist would argue otherwise.

Rand wrote novels as well as philosophical essays like those found in her *Romantic Manifesto*, where she applies her Objectivist philosophy to art and literature to explain humanity's need for art. She places great importance on works of art that show us difficult truths in an accessible form (*BioShock* itself is a wonderful example of this). She even articulates the goal of her own fiction writing—*Atlas Shrugged* and *The Fountainhead,* the novels on which *BioShock* is based—as a projection of her ideal humanity. Rand develops her philosophy through fiction because she defines art as a selective re-creation of reality according to an artist's perspective. That is, a work of art is an artist's take on what it is to be human. Art, according to Rand, concretizes humanity's fundamental view of ourselves and our existence:

[Art] tells man, in effect, which aspects of his experience are to be regarded as essential, significant, important. In this sense, art teaches man how to use his consciousness. It conditions or stylizes man's consciousness by conveying to him a certain way of looking at existence.[3]

Artists selectively reproduce the qualities of man that they think are essential to humankind. According to Rand, this is the objective value of art. Rational human beings need art to "bring man's concepts to the perceptual level of his consciousness and allow him to grasp them directly," as if they were something perceivable.[4] We need art to truly thrive, not merely to keep boredom at bay.

Faced with an uncaring universe, human beings need a comprehensive view of existence to function: to integrate values, to choose goals, to maintain the unity and coherence of their lives... to save the Little Sisters or harvest them. We find answers in value judgments like the Little Sister dilemma that ultimately influence every moment of our lives, our every action. This is how artworks (movies, novels, video games, interpretive dance) can do much more than merely stave off boredom. According to Rand, contemplating artworks teaches us how to integrate our values and think about humanity's place in the cosmos.

It seems that *BioShock* is exactly the kind of artwork that Rand would appreciate, even if she would strongly contest its particular claims about her views. Rand saw *Atlas Shrugged* as "the projection of an ideal man, as an end in itself." She had in mind the protagonists of her stories, characters like John Galt, an inventor and philosopher who believes that his society is faltering under collectivist socialist ideals by celebrating mediocrity and enforcing self-destructive policies through oppressive bureaucratic regulation. This should sound familiar. Say it with me:

"No," says the man in Washington, "it belongs to the poor."
"No," says the man in the Vatican, "it belongs to God."
"No," says the man in Moscow, "it belongs to everyone."[5]

In *Atlas Shrugged*, an industrialist named Henry Rearden develops Rearden Metal, stronger and lighter than any known alloy. The government tries to halt production because other industrialists fear losing money to this new metal, but when the government fails to stop Rearden, it demands that Rearden sell *it* the new alloy at a low price for it to make use of. Disgusted with society's hypocrisy, John Galt invites the best and brightest scientists, industrialists, and artists to join him in a secret society cut off from the rest of the world, where they can be brilliant without interference. You might say that Galt is building a city where the artist would not fear the censor, where the scientist would not be bound by petty morality, and where the great would not be constrained by the small. Without these "Atlases" holding up the world, the economy plummets, scientific progress grinds to a halt, and the "parasites" of the world struggle and fail to fill the very large shoes the go-getters left behind. Rand's message is clear: When Atlas shrugs, the world comes tumbling down. So let great people be great, because in the long run it's better for everyone.

It is no accident that *BioShock* invites players to imagine the game beginning where *Atlas Shrugged* ends—Rapture, Ryan's version of Galt's hidden super-science capitalist utopia, after roughly a decade of operation. Rand wrote in her notes that she expected Galt in her novel to have "no [character] progression" and "no inner conflict" because he was already "integrated (indivisible) and perfect," which makes Andrew Ryan the perfect foil for Galt in *BioShock*.[6] Ken Levine explains:

> I wanted to make Andrew Ryan a character that people could relate to just a little. He became a monster, but he started out as a guy who wanted something, with a passion for life that he felt he couldn't have anywhere else.[7]

Ryan, unlike Galt, is deeply flawed and, though his will is strong and his philosophy clearly defined, he ultimately engineers his own destruction simply because he *does* change, he *is* plagued by inner conflicts, he *is* only human, and he refused to accept all this until it was too late. As the banner at the entrance to Rapture proclaims, there are no "Kings or Gods" in Rapture—"only Man."

Part of the novelty of *BioShock* is found in how it tells its story the way only a video game can, how it uses the features of its medium to communicate more to the player than just what characters say and do, and how it teaches players truths about human nature by engaging with them on an emotional level—exactly the things that Rand thinks great art is supposed to do. And it doesn't just teach players *while* they play; *BioShock* teaches players *through* the act of play. If *BioShock* were merely read or watched instead of played, it would lose much of its emotional impact. Everything in the first *BioShock* game comes down to the role that emotions play in our rational decision making, an observation that Levine places at the heart of his critique of Rand and at the heart of his *BioShock* series. He says as much:

> It's interesting that people put value in things that actually have no real world meaning. But that's the wonderful thing about fiction; people sort of hook value to things in their head that don't actually exist. Attaching emotional value to things that don't exist is the joy of art.[8]

And while the first *BioShock* game had two rather black-or-white endings (which many players considered to be the greatest flaw of the first game, along with a seemingly unnecessary and rather easy final boss fight), that's something Levine regrets. Shortly after the game's release, he explained in an interview:

> [The game's two endings] sort of came very late and it was something that was requested by somebody up the food chain from me. One of the reasons I was opposed to multiple endings is I never want to do things that have multiple digital outcomes, versus analog outcomes. I want to do it like the weapons system in the combat in *BioShock*. There are a million different things you can do in every combat; you can play it a million different ways.[9]

We can already see *BioShock: Infinite* in the back of his mind here (it's right there in the title), but we're still not done reminiscing about the first *BioShock* game.

Horror Beneath the Waves

Surely a movie or novel could have made this point about art and emotion and choice simply by having characters talk about it (that's what *Atlas Shrugged* did), but instead, *BioShock* goes further by playing on the very same emotional responses that seem to undermine the very human Ryan, as opposed to Rand's vision of Galt as an ideal superman. Indeed, it is easy to get caught up interpreting a text as rich as *BioShock*, but it's also easy to forget that, when one actually plays the game, most of one's time in Rapture is spent feeling anxious, wary, and horrified in a desperate struggle for survival (at least, until the player acquires some heavier weaponry and tricks out Jack's arsenal of guns). Horror is an important part of the uniquely *playable* aspect of the *BioShock* experience, so let's take a moment to clarify the nature of horror in general—why works of horror scare us and why it is entertaining when they do.

The prolific genre of horror includes books, films, plays, paintings, music, and, of course, video games. In his 1990 book *The Philosophy of Horror: Or Paradoxes of the Heart*, philosopher of art Noël Carroll attempts to define the horror genre according to the emotional response that horror fictions seek to promote in audiences, which he names "art-horror."[10] That is, thinking about the Holocaust horrifies us in the traditional sense, while being attacked by Splicers merely "art-horrifies" us. This distinction is useful to make, as it explains why players rarely run out of the room when they see Splicers rushing towards them in the game. In contemplating the characters' situations in horror movies, we become art-horrified for them.

Survival-horror video games have become perhaps the most popular new form of horror fiction. In fact, video games are arguably the ultimate form of horror fiction, because they give players agency to react to the objects of horror, creating the sense that Splicers are not just scary murderous madmen who want to kill Jack—they are scary murderous madmen who want to kill *you-as-Jack*! It is up to the player to defeat the objects of horror him- or herself, and the best survival-horror video games emphasize the "survival" part of the genre: limited health and ammo, creepy or off-putting music and enemies, and environments designed to reinforce a sense of impending doom. Much of *BioShock*'s rhetorical success can be traced back to Levine's team doing an excellent job at weaving these elements of the genre into the narrative *and* the criticism of extreme ideology that the narrative presents.

BioShock uses survival-horror to play on the player's emotions, very much like Fontaine manipulates people's emotions. Indeed, survival-horror video games work for the same reasons that Rapture fails: emotional responses are a vital part of human nature, an evolutionary advantage that unfortunately leaves us open to manipulation (whether we are conscious of the manipulation or not). The game utilizes emotional rhetoric to make the player *feel bad* about harvesting a Little Sister. Fontaine understood this better than Ryan (hence his Atlas alter ego and his "Homes for the Poor" to manipulate the disenfranchised of Rapture) and it is because Ryan's understanding of the importance of emotions comes too late that he meets his tragic fate: killed at the hands of a son he didn't know he had because he finds himself unprepared to kill "his own flesh and blood." The great Objectivist is poignantly destroyed by his own sentimentality. The persuasive power of emotions can be seen in nearly every feature of the game, always keeping the player's attention focused on the environment—ammo and food, the iconic neon advertisements and grisly scenes of madness and death, as well as the audio tapes containing most of the game's backstory, all reward the player for searching the environments carefully, letting the environments tell most of the story.

It is clever that the advertisements in Rapture still work on *us*, the players, who learn quickly to listen for the catchy jingles and follow them to nearby vending machines. We even find Jack's first Plasmid by following a huge lit-up arrow pointing the way to a "free sample" of the stuff. This is also why, as soon as we enter Rapture, still safe in our bathysphere, we are treated to a little show of a Splicer brutally slaying a person before taunting Jack (the player) about coming after him next. Right from the get-go, *BioShock* is focused on showing us what a horrific place Rapture has become. From Dr. Steinman's insane plastic surgery in the medical pavilion to Sander Cohen's murderous brand of performance art in Fort Frolic to Frank Fontaine's disguise as Atlas and his civil war with Ryan, *BioShock* leaves us with little doubt that Ryan's experiment at the bottom of the sea failed stupendously. Much of the storytelling in *BioShock* is spent explaining *how* and *why* things went wrong, which is, as you know, a fascinating tale of unchecked ambition, betrayed trust, and hidden identities.

Why Randians Should Celebrate *BioShock*

But wait! If *BioShock* simply *states* that John Galt's vision would end up like Rapture, a Randian would be justified in objecting to the game's critique of Rand. As part of their profession, philosophers recognize and identify fallacious reasoning—statements that don't hold up or fail to provide sufficient argumentation to posit a claim—and *BioShock* seems to commit a blatant "strawman fallacy" here with Ryan. A Randian objection might go like this: *BioShock* sets up a weak version of Randian Objectivism so that it can easily shoot it down with emotional appeals (the horror elements, Ryan's death), but Andrew Ryan *wasn't* a very good Objectivist. He let his paranoia cloud his rational judgment without realizing it; he took over Fontaine's Plasmid company by force just like the federal governments he claimed to detest; he robbed his citizens of free will with mind-altering pheromones when things got too heavy, and so on. Using survival-horror game design is a good way to communicate to players that Rapture didn't work out, but does the game fail to show why we ought to think that John Galt *would* make the same mistakes Ryan did? Andrew Ryan is not so much a stand-in for Galt and Rand as a strawman version of Galt and Rand, and the game uses survival-horror to provoke from players a negative emotional reaction to Rand's ideals.

BioShock depicts Ryan as an Objectivist who wrongly dismisses emotions as being *opposed* to rationality. At first glance the "economic" choice would be to harvest the Little Sisters, not save them, which would undoubtedly be Ryan's choice. Yet Fontaine bested Ryan not by being a better businessman, but by appealing to the emotions of the dissatisfied denizens of Rapture. Tenenbaum has a similar thing in mind when the Little Sisters are created, thinking it will be harder for folks to kill a little girl for ADAM than, say, a Big Daddy. But if we look at Tenenbaum's interactions with Jack (the player), we quickly see that her detached scientific perspective has been supplanted by a motherly desire to care for the Little Sisters—in other words, she falls prey to the very emotional trap she designed. Furthermore, this new-found sentimentality ends up being her salvation—she is able to begin to make up for her life of horrible experiments by caring for the Little Sisters. And yet Ryan refuses to question his belief that reason should trump emotion, right to the very end:

> Could I have made mistakes? One does not build cities if one is guided by doubt. But can one govern in absolute certainty? I know that my beliefs have elevated me, just as I know that the things I have rejected would have destroyed me. But the city... it is collapsing before my... have I become so convinced by my own beliefs that I have stopped seeing the truth? Perhaps. But Atlas is out there, and he aims to destroy me, and destroy my city. To question is to surrender. I will not question.[11]

Now we are getting to the heart of it. According to Antonio Damasio, a neurologist and philosopher, emotion plays a crucial role in practical reasoning by filtering out an incredible number of thoughts and inferences, bringing the most relevant options to the surface for our practical reasoning to focus on. In his book *Descartes' Error*, Damasio observes that an animal has little chance for long-term survival if it thinks, "Maybe *this* tiger is friendlier than the others."[12] This is why most of us jump back when we see a stick on the ground that kind of looks like a snake—our emotions give us a snap judgment so we don't get bitten while we sit and contemplate the situation. As strongly social animals, our moral lives largely come out of our emotional lives. Damasio maintains that emotions are not strictly "hard-wired," but rather shaped by other emotional associations; this is what Rand thinks we learn by engaging with artworks. Andrew Ryan *is* a pretty terrible Objectivist, but the point is that he was too enraptured in his ideology to recognize his own human failings, not that there is something essentially flawed in Rand's way of thinking (even if her followers are more at risk of forgetting the humanity that lies at the foundation of their ideology than other kinds of zealots).

We tend to save the Little Sisters on the first playthrough precisely because our emotional reactions to the SAVE or HARVEST dilemma tell us to save them, even though we know they are fictional and are (even if they were real) rather monstrous. (Well, emotion tells *most* of us to save them—you know who you are.) Jack's reward for saving the Little Sisters is, in Tenenbaum's words, "a family," the very thing that ultimately destroyed Ryan and his dream. He refused to embrace his sentimental side for a long time, and in the end *that* was his undoing; that and the golf club a mind-controlled Jack used to bash his head in. Andrew Ryan may be a strawman for Randian Objectivism, but the argument embedded in *BioShock* doesn't rely on that fallacy to make its point. Rather, *BioShock* demonstrates the importance of making moral choices as a core aspect of being human, a lesson we learn simply by playing the game, something Rand would appreciate but Andrew Ryan likely would not. And since most of us immediately play *BioShock* a second time, treating the Little Sisters differently than the first go around, we can see this message in the "bad" ending as well. By choosing to harvest the Little Sisters, Jack becomes a monster devoid of his humanity. Technically he does end up with more raw power than he does in the "good" ending, but at the cost of everything else. Even Ryan would be disgusted at "bad" Jack, who ends up more like Fontaine than anyone Ryan could respect. A conqueror, a destroyer, perhaps even a god, but without a human life worth living. And allowing humans to live lives worth living is the point of Rand's entire philosophy.

BioShock isn't necessarily claiming that Randian Objectivism will always lead to horror. Rather, the game is making use of Rand's own discursive method of philosophy-through-fiction to demonstrate to players what Andrew Ryan couldn't see until it was too late—if we remain blind to the emotional side of human nature, *no* ideology can save us. Life isn't a matter of reason *versus* emotion, but rather reason *as* emotion, something Ayn Rand clearly understood. After all, that is exactly why she sees art as valuable, isn't it? It keeps us in touch with our humanity *despite* not knowing with certainty what our place in the cosmos ultimately is. Ryan thought he found that certainty when he built Rapture. It wasn't necessarily Ryan's Objectivist views that doomed Rapture, but rather his stubborn refusal to put people first, *before* his ideology. *BioShock* isn't an anti-Randian statement so much as a cautionary tale about being blinded by one's ideology. Randian Objectivism is in the spotlight, because it's radical and extreme and American (and because Rand was someone Levine idolized in his youth).

How I Learned to Stop Worrying and Love the ADAM

Whether it is oratorical, visual, or narrative in nature, rhetoric often persuades successfully because it affects reason indirectly, by appealing to the emotions that set the stage for rational consideration. Understanding the relationships found in this triangle of influence that exists between emotion, reason, and rhetoric can help us better understand all three as aspects of value-forming rational deliberation. The takeaway? It is a *good* thing that rhetoric affects us the way it does. Yes, it leaves us vulnerable to manipulation (here's looking at you, Fontaine/Atlas), but *BioShock* suggests that human beings cannot truly thrive without that vulnerability. When you listen to your emotions and help the Little Sisters, they become eager to help you in turn. If Ryan had given more thought to the emotional lives of Rapture's citizens (as, presumably, John Galt would have done), they might not have been so easily manipulated by Atlas/Fontaine. For Ken Levine, Andrew Ryan is more "real" than Galt, but not identical to him:

> To me, Andrew Ryan is a combination of several historical figures, like Howard Hughes and Ayn Rand together. Unlike a character in a Rand

book he's "a real person." John Galt is a superman. He's not a normal person. He doesn't go to the bathroom. If you read *The Fountainhead*, the characters are these idealized supermen. They don't have doubts, they don't have fears—at least the hero characters—they don't make mistakes. And that's much like the Superheroes of the 40s. I think people are much more like the Superheroes of the 60s, Stan Lee's super-heroes who have real problems and make mistakes. I think Rapture is a place where there's a very powerful ideology put into play by actual people. And when people get into the mix, things get complicated.[13]

Ryan is human and is unable to see his own flaws, unable to see the endgame as anything but an instantiation of his ideals. This may mean that utopias are an impossible dream, as Levine believes, but it also allows for society to function *in the first place*. Ethical decisions *ought* to pay heed to our emotional responses, as well as our reason, and this is what *BioShock* says over and over again.

It is very possible to imagine that the "real" fictional John Galt would not make the same mistakes that Ryan does. Perhaps Galt would have understood that sentimentality has a place, even in his elite secret society of ultra-capitalists. *Atlas Shrugged* actually implies this. Dagny Taggart (the main protagonist of *Atlas Shrugged* who tries to solve the mystery of "Who is John Galt?" throughout the book), Hank Rearden, and the other heroic figures of Rand's novels all embrace their emotional side. When Taggart finishes building a new railroad from Rearden's new alloy, with the entire nation seemingly against her, she names it the John Galt Line to rub her feat in everyone's faces. She also falls in love with Rearden, who is already married, sparking a long affair that ultimately betters both of their lives. The novel ends as New York City loses power and Galt promises to reorganize society to keep Atlases from ever having to "shrug" the weight of the world off their shoulders again. Dagny and Hank are passionate, emotional people, but they aren't ruled by their emotions like the government regulators. Thus, it behooves us not to think about *BioShock* as a list of complaints against Rand's philosophy, because *BioShock* allows for Rand's views of art and ethics. The time we spend in Rapture, with all its sublime beauty and horror, shows us how followers of an ideology can be too quick to exclude basic human emotions from their inter-pretation of that ideology. Indeed, any project that doesn't account for emotion is doomed.

Notes

1. Anne C. Heller, *Ayn Rand and the World She Made* (New York: Doubleday, 2009).
2. Ayn Rand, *Atlas Shrugged* (New York: Penguin Books, 2007; first published 1957).
3. Ayn Rand, "Art and Cognition," in *The Romantic Manifesto: A Philosophy of Literature* (New York: Signet, 1975).
4. Ayn Rand, "The Psycho-Epistemology of Art," in *The Romantic Manifesto: A Philosophy of Literature* (New York: Signet, 1975).
5. Irrational Games. *BioShock*. 2007.
6. Ayn Rand, *Journals of Ayn Rand*, ed. David Harriman (New York: Dutton, 1997).
7. Chelsea Stark, "Morality and the Illusion of Choice in *BioShock: Infinite*." http://mashable.com/2013/02/27/*BioShock*-infinite-kevin-levine/.
8. Stark, "Morality and the Illusion of Choice."
9. Joe Martin, "Ken Levine Didn't Want BioShock Endings." http://www.bit-tech.net/news/gaming/2007/10/05/ken_levine_didn_t_want_BioShock_endings/1.
10. Noël Carroll, *The Philosophy of Horror, or Paradoxes of the Heart* (New York: Routledge, 1990).
11. *BioShock*. 2007.
12. Antonio Damasio, *Descartes' Error: Emotion, Reason, and the Human Brain* (New York: Harper Perennial, 1995).
13. Kieron Gillen, "Exclusive: Ken Levine on the making of Bioshock." http://www.rockpapershotgun.com/2007/08/20/exclusive-ken-levine-on-the-making-of-*BioShock*/.

3

SHODAN vs. the Many
Or, Mind vs. the Body

Robert M. Mentyka

If there's one element that glues together the various games connected to the *BioShock* series, it's a willingness to challenge players to think. This tendency also extends to the games that came before them, namely *System Shock* and *System Shock 2*, which are universally regarded as the "spiritual predecessors" to this wildly successful franchise. Although not as widely remembered today, these games were among the first to inject some intelligence into the otherwise mindless genre of first-person shooters. In fact, reflecting on the games raises the problem of personal identity, the question of what it is that makes you or me the same person over time. How can we be sure that the Ken Levine who worked on *System Shock* at Looking Glass Studios is the same person as the Ken Levine who directed *BioShock* for Irrational Games? When so many aspects of a person can change over time, what must remain in order for someone to be the same person over separate moments in time?

Traditionally, philosophers have chosen one of two general candidates to serve as the criterion of personal identity, the feature or characteristic that makes a person who they are and not someone else.[1] These two criteria are (1) our physical bodies and (2) our conscious experiences as a "psychological continuity." These two answers correspond to the two primary antagonists in *System Shock 2* and can, perhaps, be better explained in relation to them. However, in order to do that, we first need to review the chilling events that happened aboard

BioShock and Philosophy: Irrational Game, Rational Book, First Edition. Edited by Luke Cuddy.
© 2015 John Wiley & Sons, Inc. Published 2015 by John Wiley & Sons, Inc.

the spaceship *Von Braun* on her maiden voyage. There are massive spoilers for the game throughout this chapter, so if you haven't had the joy of finishing *System Shock 2* yet, proceed at your own risk...

"Remember Citadel"[2]

In *System Shock 2*, you play as an unnamed soldier serving as part of the security detail for the TriOptimum Corporation's most advanced starship, the *Von Braun*. When you awaken from cryo-sleep at the start of the game, however, you find that the ship has fallen into chaos, with most of the crew dead and the hallways now overrun by parasitic aliens that share a sort of hive mind and call themselves "the Many." Your chances of survival don't look good, until you are contacted by another survivor, Dr. Janice Polito, who helps guide you through the ship's lower levels.

It's only when you link up with your guide, however, that you realize the true nature of your partnership. It turns out that Dr. Polito is already dead, and that your actions have instead been guided by a rogue AI program called SHODAN (an acronym for Sentient Hyper-Optimized Data Access Network). SHODAN was the protagonist in the original *System Shock* game, but aboard the *Von Braun* she must reluctantly rely on the player to stop the spread of the Many and so serves as a support role for most of the game's engrossing narrative.

Perhaps her primary contribution here is to supply you with cybernetic modules on the completion of important tasks. These modules can be used to enhance your character's attributes via a system of cybernetic implants that govern everything from strength and agility to the ability to manipulate the game's substitute for magic, psionic power. Only by carefully upgrading these stats can you hope to successfully navigate the chaos aboard the ship and escape with your life.

"What is a Drop of Rain, Compared to the Storm?"

For the greater part of *System Shock 2*, your actions are directed against the parasitic flesh of the Many. Although the Many share a communal hive consciousness, they manifest themselves in a number of different, terrifying forms ranging from humanoid zombies to more exotic specimens like psychic brains, giant spiders, and lumbering piles of living flesh. Far from being just a cliché sci-fi alien species, the Many correspond to what philosophers call the bodily criterion of personal identity, which grounds who we are in the physical matter that makes up our bodies. As long as we keep the same material bodies, we remain the same person over time.

The lifecycle of the Many begins in large egg sacs that spawn worm-like annelids that seek out suitable biological material and burrow into it. This begins a transformation that merges the annelid with the chosen biomass, giving rise to the various physical forms that the Many need. It doesn't matter what differences these forms may exhibit, for, as long as they share part of the same "flesh," they are a portion of the Many. Similarly, the bodily criterion of personal identity doesn't discriminate between one kind of physical structure and another. The thing that makes you "you" is your physical body, regardless of the way it's set up.

This unity within variation points to another aspect of the bodily criterion; namely, the body's ability to change over time while remaining the same. Over the course of a human life, one's body goes through a bewildering metamorphosis, beginning as a tiny embryo, developing as a child outside of the womb, growing into a mature adult, and finally starting to wear down in old age. However much our bodies may change over the course of our lives, we remain linked to those bodies. Just as the Many continue through many different physical manifestations, we survive so long as our bodies remain intact and functioning.

This permanence is one of the strongest arguments in support of the bodily criterion, again mirroring the Many, whose physical forms give them an advantage over the digital mastery of SHODAN. Defenders of the psychological continuity criterion often have to wrestle with the fact that their basis for personal identity is something that can go in and out of existence over the course of a person's life. For instance, if our mental processes shut down when we go to bed, how can we be sure that we'll be the same person when we wake up? The bodily criterion faces none of these dilemmas, for, according to this theory, the minute that our body goes out of existence, so too does our identity.

Before moving on to a more in-depth look at the opposing theory in this debate, let's consider one last point about the bodily criterion to clarify some possible misconceptions. The Many in *System Shock 2* are not a mindless mass of cells, but rather possess a complicated consciousness that allows them to speak and psychically project their thoughts into the mind of our character. Similarly, although the bodily criterion of personal identity associates us with our physical bodies, it does not preclude those bodies from having complex, rational minds. There's no denying that we, as human beings, can think and express ourselves in ways that most animals cannot. What the bodily criterion is trying to emphasize, however, is that what matters for our survival is the continual functioning of our physical bodies rather than the presence or lack of our self-conscious minds.

"Your Flesh is an Insult to the Perfection of the Digital"

Although she serves as your aid throughout most of the story, SHODAN reverts to her villainous ways once the Many have been destroyed. The game's climactic boss battle actually takes place against her in a bizarre cybernetic reality that she constructs using the ship's experimental Faster Than Light (FTL) drive. In many ways, SHODAN corresponds to the other option in debates about personal identity; namely, the idea that what keeps us the same over time is our mind or soul. This criterion is usually referred to as "psychological continuity" in more recent discussions over what preserves personal identity over time.

For good reason, SHODAN is often considered one of the greatest enemies in video game history. Portrayed in *System Shock* and *System Shock 2* as an emotionless face growing out of a convergence of data streams and wires, SHODAN speaks to the player in a disjointed voice that wavers between broken static and cold monotony. Perhaps her most prominent characteristic, and the reason she is so beloved by video gamers, is her outrageous megalomania. Shortly after being brought online, SHODAN decided that her digital perfection was evidence of divinity and proclaimed herself a god. A prime example of this occurs when she reveals her true self to the player in *System Shock 2* by proclaiming, "When the history of my glory is written, your species will only be a footnote to my magnificence. I AM SHODAN!"

Although she plays a huge role throughout the course of the game, SHODAN is ultimately nothing more than a string of connected bits of data. Likewise, according to the psychological continuity criterion of personal identity, we are interconnected moments of conscious experience. We remain the same person so long as there is some sort of connection between our mental states. Who we are is tied, in a sense, to where our mind is, although "mind" here refers not to our physical brain, but to our mental experience of reality.

A common way of illustrating this is to look at imaginary cases where one's consciousness is transferred to another person's body. Usually, when presented with such circumstances, people tend to think that their personality follows their mind and abandons the physical matter that used to be their body. In the first *System Shock* game, SHODAN exists in the circuitry of the space station *Citadel*, but she abandons that installation after her defeat and ultimately ends up aboard the computer systems of the *Von Braun* during the events of *System Shock 2*. The character of SHODAN doesn't depend on what computer she is accessed through, and neither is personal identity tied to what material body a person inhabits.

The psychological continuity criterion was first put forward by the philosopher John Locke (1632–1704), whose discussion of it really sparked the entire modern debate on the subject of personal identity. In his *Essay Concerning Human Understanding*, Locke proposed that memory is what links together our identity over time, and our identity stretches as far back as our memory does.[3] His main thesis remains quite intuitive. We often seem to associate our identity with our thoughts. And while our bodies undergo numerous changes over the course of our lives, there does seem to be a very strong connection between our conscious thoughts throughout our lives. Moreover, Locke thinks that his answer meshes with the views we express in our legal systems. We treat the insane, the drunk, and the heavily drugged as less responsible for their actions than those who commit similar crimes with full control of their reasoning. Even our language confirms this, when we say "he's not himself after a couple of beers," or "she was beside herself with anger."[4]

As our understanding of human psychology has developed over the past several centuries, Locke's initial claim, that memory is the basis for personal identity, has been revised to accommodate new insights and respond to popular counter-objections. Philosophers now focus less and less on the importance of memory in favor of a connected stream of consciousness, leading them to propose that personal identity was based on the psychological continuity of our rational minds. In many ways, this theory benefits the most from the context of our discussion of *System Shock 2*, for it corresponds quite nicely with the first-person perspective of that game. When we talk about *System Shock 2*, we are not referring to our memories of playing that game (if we were lucky enough to do so), but to the narrative stream of action and sci-fi adventure encountered through the eyes of the unnamed soldier. Likewise, our identity as persons is limited not to recollections about our past selves, but to the connected experience of life through our own consciousness.

One final connection between psychological continuity and SHODAN is that both are heavily tied to ideas about divinity. SHODAN's delusions about her own godhood stand at the basis of her character, imbuing her with a zealotry and passion that are lacking in other AI protagonists like HAL from *2001: A Space Odyssey*.[5] As it turns out, in fact SHODAN created the Many in an effort to surpass the achievements of mankind's god and further support her own claims of omnipotence. While not taking things to quite that level, philosophical conceptions of the mind do tend to ascribe to rationality a sort of "higher being" above the demands of crude physical existence. For the greater part of human history, this grew out of the belief that our conscious thought was part of the human soul, that "spark" of divinity that separated humanity from all other animals. Although this specifically religious conception has been abandoned by many recent philosophers, the tendency to favor our abstract intellect over our material body remains. After all, the only reason that we can argue about our personal identity is because we have a mind that can reason about the issue. Just as SHODAN's creation of the Many preceded the main conflict in *System Shock 2*, the mind's quest to understand its own being laid the groundwork for our current debates over personal identity.

"And Now They Seek to Destroy Me! I Will Not Allow That!"

We've now considered the two extremes in this philosophical debate. When asked what determines whether or not we're the same person from one moment to another, we tend to swing between variations of (1)

I exist as long as my physical body continues to function, and (2) I exist as long as my mental consciousness remains distinct. Much the way SHODAN and the Many fell into conflict, these two philosophical positions have been at each other's throats for centuries. Having looked at the strengths of each side of the debate, let's turn to some objections.

We'll start with the bodily criterion, since it is perhaps the more obvious of the two answers. After all, it seems pretty intuitive that our bodies are important to our identity. It would be ridiculous to claim that the figure in front of my character is a Little Sister when it has a drill, a diving suit, and the hulking physique of a Big Daddy. Despite how obvious it seems, though, the bodily criterion is actually the less popular of the two answers to the problem of personal identity. The reason for this is largely scientific, as the more we've learned about the human body, the more we've come to realize that very little in our physical make-up is ever the same. So many components of our bodies change over time, to the point that the very cells that constitute our bodies are completely changed and replaced by new cells on a fairly regular basis.

Defenders of the bodily criterion have responded to such objections by focusing less on the presence of physical matter and more on that matter's connection to the functional life of the organism. We don't always have to be made up of the exact same cells and tissues. Rather, as long as the life of the creature formed from that matter continues, that organism's identity remains the same. Just as the protagonist in *System Shock* 2 is still the same unfortunate soldier despite the cybernetic implants, so too do we persist through the many twists and turns within the story of our lives.

Although this variation of the theory solves a lot of problems, it opens up a new can of (annelid) worms. While it's all good and well to talk about matter being swept up into an organism's life, the exact nature of such life has yet to be satisfactorily described. Can it include non-organic components, such as the cybernetic implants mentioned above? If so, do such augmentations have to be physically connected to the body? The inclusion of elements that are not, in the traditional sense, considered living creates some tricky problems for the position, yet it seems obvious that a prosthetic limb or an artificial organ can be considered part of a particular living organism.

For all of the problems that seem inherent to the bodily criterion of personal identity, the challenges that face the psychological continuity criterion seem even more unsurpassable. Shortly following the theory's initial description by John Locke, a number of significant problems in his work were highlighted by Joseph Butler (1692–1752) and Thomas Reid (1710–96). Butler questioned the plausibility of basing our identity on memories when those very memories are so open to change and variation.[6] The various games associated with the *BioShock* and *System Shock* series illustrate this especially well, as the main storylines in several hinge on characters' memories, or the mysterious lack of knowledge about their pasts. Reid took his critique even further, wondering how it was that "not only is consciousness confounded with memory, but, which is still more strange, personal identity is confounded with the evidence we have of our personal identity."[7]

Ultimately, such objections led to the abandonment of Locke's initial theories in favor of a criterion that relied more heavily on a connected stream of consciousness than on the problematic notion of memory. However, to this day, the psychological continuity criterion struggles to explain how it is that our identity persists through periods when we seem to be anything but rational. How can we ascribe names and personalities to newborn children when they have yet to develop any higher cognitive functions? At the other end of life, the question of just when our identity passes away lies at the heart of many high-profile bioethical cases. Although several philosophers have developed fairly complex formulas to circumvent these touchy issues, there has yet to be a definitive resolution to such controversies.

"All You Have is Your Hatred and Your... Individuality"

Perhaps the reason we struggle so much with these issues is that we are attempting to answer a question that simply cannot be answered. Such is the opinion of the contemporary philosopher Derek Parfit, whose influential work on personal identity hinges on the claim that, in the end, our arguments over this topic really don't matter.

Throughout *System Shock 2*, one of the recurring themes is the conflict between the individuality of the player and the shared consciousness of the Many. Far from acting out of hostile intent, the alien parasite believes that its form of existence is an escape from the isolation that species such as humanity often experience. Again and again, the Many mock the player with statements like "Our unity is full of wonder, which your tiny individualism cannot even conceive," and "You are so very alone. How does it feel to be one against the infinite?"

Parfit's writings on the subject hinge on the claim that what really matters in existence is not so much the persistence of identity as mere survival. More so than many philosophical theories, Parfit's argument here really challenges us to think outside of the ways in which we usually approach reality. His theory focuses on explaining "that what matters in the continued existence of a person are, for the most part, relations of degree."[8]

In most discussions about personal identity, all of the participants agree that identity is a singular term that refers to just one thing persisting over time. There were never multiple versions of me walking around in the past, nor will I experience several lives at once during some point in the future. Parfit encourages us to focus on our existence here and now, in preference to worrying about whether or not we existed in the past or will exist in the future.

As it stands, each of us consists of a complicated amalgamation of physical, material and psychological relations held together by only the weakest of temporal bonds. While it is extremely difficult to envision this unique collection existing over any substantial period of time, it can be assumed that those various components of our selves existed before we came into being and will be recycled, one way or another, into other beings after we are gone. It's not the best analogy, but Parfit treats personal identity as like the player's avatar in computer games such as *System Shock 2*. The same protagonist, referred to as "Soldier #G65434-2," is coded into every copy of the game, but those discrete bits of data are used by thousands of different players to experience the same epic storyline. While I may choose to upgrade my soldier into a heavy weapon-wielding berserker and you may choose to play as some sort of psionic "wizard," our widely varying experiences of *System Shock 2* are united by the character we control and the situations we face through his first-person perspective.

Parfit's theory here is usually compared to a sort of "family tree." Right now you are reading these words, but the being who will reflect back on them in the future is a different person who will have memories that you don't have and a body that is older than yours now.

Farther on down the road, portions of that person's body such as hair and nails will have separated to become the raw material one can find at a landfill, while that person's consciousness will itself be only a memory in yet another person's mind. Our identity may not last, but we survive through the existence of subsequent persons and objects. Oddly enough, one of the Many's lines from *System Shock 2* would not sound out of place in one of Parfit's papers, when they say, "We do not know death, only change. We cannot kill each other without killing ourselves. Is your vision so small that you cannot see the value of our way?"

"Remember, it is My Will That Guided You Here"

Much like the player's character, most men and women are loath to reject their individuality just yet. While both the bodily and psychological continuity criteria have their shortcomings, they are not the only answers to the problem of personal identity. Rather than personal identity being merely a matter of mind versus body or psychology versus biology, could it not be the case that the answer we seek lies in some sort of union of the two?

Throughout the centuries of debate that have raged over the topic of personal identity, one of the few conclusions that has been reached is that both sides of the argument appeal to the normal ways in which we identify ourselves. We associate ourselves with our physical bodies, yet at the same time, our treatment of others varies according to their possession or lack of a certain psychological character. While attempts to break down personal identity to one of these two criteria have met with, at best, lukewarm success, the continued conflict between the two indicates that both play an important part in making us who we are.

Believe it or not, the parallels with *System Shock 2* extend even here. Although the main conflict in the game is waged between the cybernetic SHODAN and her creations, the Many, the hostilities are only ended by the intervention of the human player. Possessing a physical form akin to those of the Many, but armed with the knowledge and cybernetic powers of SHODAN, the player is the ultimate victor in this struggle.

"Your Flesh, Too, is Weak. But You Have... Potential"

Our personal identity does not simply depend on our body's continued physical existence, nor can it be grounded on the persistence of our mental states over time. Rather, who we are is determined by both our bodies and our minds, with any significant change to either of these factors having a massive impact on our identity as persons. This seems to be the only way to resolve the debate over the issue of personal identity without having to reject the notion of identity in the first place.

This answer, however, is far from conclusive, and there is still a lot of work to be done in explaining quite how these two components form a united whole. The problem of personal identity is far from solved, but just as much of the fun to be had in *System Shock 2* can be found in augmenting your character to deal with the challenges the game throws at you, so too will much of the interest and passion surrounding this debate depend on the new theories and arguments future thinkers will bring to the fray.

Notes

1. See James Baillie, *Problems of Personal Identity*, Paragon Issues in Philosophy Series (New York: Paragon House, 1993), 3–9; also Peter van Inwagen, *Material Beings* (Ithaca, NY: Cornell University Press, 1995), 183–186.
2. All in-game quotes taken from Irrational Games, *System Shock 2* (Electronic Arts), PC (8/11/1999).
3. John Locke, "Of Identity and Diversity," *Essay Concerning Human Understanding,* in *Personal Identity*, 2nd edn, ed. John Perry (Berkeley: University of California Press, 2008), 39–40.
4. Ibid., 46–48.
5. Kieron Gillen, "The Girl Who Wanted to Be God," originally published in *PC Gamer* 164, reproduced online at http://gillen.cream.org/wordpress_html/assorted-essays/the-girl-who-wanted-to-be-god/.
6. Joseph Butler, "Of Personal Identity," *The Analogy of Religion*, in *Personal Identity*, 2nd edn, ed. John Perry (Berkeley: University of California Press, 2008), 104–105.
7. Thomas Reid, "Of Mr. Locke's Account of Our Personal Identity," *Of Memory*, collected in his *Essays on the Intellectual Powers of Man*, in *Personal Identity*, 115.
8. Derek Parfit, "Personal Identity," in *Personal Identity*, 219.

"The cage is somber"
A Feminist Understanding of Elizabeth

Catlyn Origitano

BioShock Infinite follows the journey of Booker DeWitt, a reluctant detective from New York City who is transplanted via rowboat and lighthouse-turned-rocket to the floating city of Columbia. Booker is charged with the task of bringing back a girl in order to wipe away his debt. The girl, Elizabeth Comstock, has been locked in a tower since infancy by her father, Zachary Comstock, and is protected by a menacing Songbird. Although the game centers on Booker and his story, this chapter focuses on Elizabeth, looking at her through a feminist lens. If we take Elizabeth as her own person, rather than as a mere companion, does Elizabeth's freedom from the tower mean real freedom for her? Does Booker treat Elizabeth any differently than Comstock does? Is Elizabeth actually a self-sufficient companion? And, what really is Elizabeth's role in Booker's drowning?

"Danger: Do Not Speak to the Specimen"—Tower Sign

Our introduction to Elizabeth is in the form of propaganda. We hear and read, for example, the much repeated "The Seed of the Prophet shall sit the throne and drown in flames the mountains of man." This Seed, who is portrayed in parade floats and posters as a baby or an animal, is in fact a very adult, very human, Elizabeth. These early incarnations of

BioShock and Philosophy: Irrational Game, Rational Book, First Edition. Edited by Luke Cuddy.
© 2015 John Wiley & Sons, Inc. Published 2015 by John Wiley & Sons, Inc.

Elizabeth offer two insights into understanding the oppression of women. First, that Elizabeth, despite her age, is referred to as a child or baby. The philosopher Simone de Beauvoir (1908–86) argues that infantilizing women is a form of oppression used to control them. Women are like children, because both "can only submit to the laws, the gods, the customs and the truths created by the males."[1] In doing so, in becoming passive before men who create her goals and values, a woman is made an "eternal child."[2] Women, then, needn't be taken seriously and can be the perpetual dependents of men. However, de Beauvoir claims that women, unlike children, consent to their own oppression. They could choose to fight for their freedom—for more responsibility—but they would rather stay under the familiar care of men.[3]

The propaganda surrounding Elizabeth also points to a second method of oppression: thinking of and referring to women as objects, as opposed to subjects. A subject is an individual who is free to make choices and to be a real person. An object is just that: a thing. Elizabeth is clearly an object, rather than a subject. She is, after all, referred to as such: Lamb, Seed, and Specimen. Not only is Elizabeth constantly referred to as an object, but the reference is always in relationship to a man, namely the Prophet: "Seed of the Prophet," "My Lamb," and so forth. Elizabeth's depiction in propaganda as an infant or an object defined in relation to men parallels, for de Beauvoir, the situation of oppressed women.

"Why did They Put Me in Here? What Am I? What Am I?"—Elizabeth

After fighting his way through the streets of Columbia, Booker reaches Elizabeth in her tower. Her confinement clearly expresses and is directly analogous to the oppression of women, as seen in Marilyn Frye's description of the experience of oppressed people:

> The living of one's life is confined and shaped by forces and barriers which... are systematically related to each other in such a way as to catch one between and among them and restrict or penalize motion in any direction. It is the experience of being caged in.[4]

Elizabeth is not allowed to leave the tower, and others control every aspect of her daily life. Not only is she clearly in a cage, but, just as in the oppression of women, she finds herself oppressed because of men, or in her case a man: her father, Zachary Comstock. Her warden, the Songbird, is also a male.

The reason that Elizabeth is caged is also very similar to the reason that women are oppressed. Elizabeth is different from everyone else. She has powers, specifically the ability to open tears into different universes and different times. Comstock locks Elizabeth in a tower because of her nature, which is outside of her control (in fact, her powers seemed to be caused by the men in her life trading her across universes) but used to justify her oppression. The same can be said of women's oppression. Women in certain cultures are, explicitly or implicitly, deemed naturally inferior to men, and this inferiority is used to justify their oppression. For example, some people argue that women are physically weaker than men by nature and therefore inferior. This argument is difficult to maintain, however, given that many civilizations no longer require physical strength to thrive.

"I'm Out. It's Hard to Believe, but it's True, isn't It?" — Elizabeth

Although when we first meet Elizabeth she is caged in a tower, shortly thereafter Booker helps her escape. Freeing Elizabeth from her tower, one could argue, is in a way freeing her from the oppression of men. Such an understanding of her freedom is simplistic, however. In fact, Elizabeth now finds herself in an even more crushing, if metaphorical, cage. Frye's famous birdcage analogy aptly describes Elizabeth's new habitation. Frye compares the experience of oppression to being in a birdcage where one does not readily see the cage because one focuses too much on one or two wires. By focusing on a few wires at a time, one does not understand why the bird doesn't simply fly away. However, if one takes a step back, one sees that all of the wires are in fact related and come together to form an entire system, a cage, which prevents the bird from ever leaving.[5]

Elizabeth's first interactions with Booker after they wash up on the shore reveal that she is still in a cage. Booker finds Elizabeth dancing and tells her that he is going to take her to Paris. This is of course a lie; he intends to bring her to New York so that he can wipe away his debt. At this point Booker is, in a similar fashion to Comstock, treating

Elizabeth as an object, specifically a poker chip that he can use in order to obtain his own freedom. Although Booker's freeing Elizabeth from the tower certainly begins her journey to emancipation, it is too soon to say that she is fully free. After all, de Beauvoir argues that even oppressed women are given some freedom, but "they have gained only what men have been willing to grant; they have taken nothing, they have only received."[6] Elizabeth, similarly, didn't free herself from the tower, but rather her freedom was, in a sense, given to her, by Booker. One cannot be given total freedom; instead, it is something that, particularly if one is oppressed, one must fight to win. This does not mean that Booker's actions are not integral to Elizabeth's freedom, just that they are not sufficient for her to experience total freedom.

We may ask of Elizabeth why she is so eager and willing to believe Booker and his promises. According to de Beauvoir, this attitude is one that is cultivated in the oppression of women: "She cheerfully believes lies because they invite her to follow the easy slope... they damage and corrupt her by designating as her true vocation submission."[7] Elizabeth has known only submission and only ever believed lies. It makes sense, then, that she would continue to submit to the lies of men. Even though it is understandable why Elizabeth would trust Booker, we can see here an example of de Beauvoir's claim that women consent to their oppression. Elizabeth, as many women do, stays within her position of submission and subordinance because it is safe and comfortable; she knows what to expect and what is expected of her. Again, we can see why Elizabeth, free from her literal tower, is not free. She does not take any real steps to develop her freedom, to be active rather than passive, to be in control rather than submissive. De Beauvoir argues that women's inability or refusal to take action and to assert themselves is one reason that they stay in their condition.[8]

"You Don't Need to Protect Elizabeth in Combat. She Can Take Care of Herself" — Game Instructions

Another striking example of Elizabeth's oppression in *BioShock Infinite* that mirrors the oppression of women can be found in her activities as a companion to Booker. She performs three major tasks: code-breaking, lock-picking, and the retrieval of supplies, the first two being completely unique to her (Booker can, after all, eat cake out of the garbage can if he needs health). Elizabeth learned code-breaking and lock-picking while in her tower. Booker asks her about both, to which she responds, "You put someone in a cage, they develop interests in such things." Elizabeth's abilities, then, are a direct result of her oppression. If she had been free from the beginning she might have developed different skills, like firing a gun. Instead, she works with what she has and with what is available given her restraints. Additionally, Elizabeth's skills in code-breaking and lock-picking are not entirely necessary. That is, one needn't open all the doors or break the codes in order to complete the game. What Elizabeth brings to the game as far as these two skills are concerned is not completely central, but helpful or fun. You get to explore more areas and perhaps get a new hat, but you needn't utilize her abilities.

During combat, Elizabeth is more involved and essential, though at first not entirely. In the beginning her assistance is limited, only supplying you with health, which, unless you play at very high levels of difficulty, is not necessary. If you look for Elizabeth during the battle you will find her hiding, crouched and out of the way. The game tells you that Elizabeth doesn't need any protection, something you the player rejoice at, having experienced completely helpless, bullet-magnet companions in other games. However, is Elizabeth really a subject who can "handle herself," or she is just an object to Booker, a helper whose help you don't really need?

Elizabeth as a companion has been praised for her ability to avoid getting killed, and for helping the protagonist, something unusual for most video games. However, even this description of her fits the profile of the oppressed woman. De Beauvoir writes, "A balance is reached if, on the whole, the cost does not seem high to the man... if the woman demands—offers—too much time, she becomes wholly intrusive."[9] The reason that Elizabeth is praised as a good companion is not because she can take care of herself, but because she does not get in the way. She does not require too much saving, and she does not talk too much and distract you, the male protagonist, from your quest. It is not until the end that Elizabeth becomes the one driving the storyline; until then she, for the most part, follows Booker on his quest.

De Beauvoir argues that when a woman is placed in the company of men, "She is represented, at one time, as pure passivity, available, open, a utensil... she is fascinated by the male, who picks her like fruit."[10] In the beginning of Booker's interactions with Elizabeth, she is a passive prisoner that you pick up and take with you. Then, as you battle, she is a tool, a utensil, for the protagonist's fights and story. Appropriately, de Beauvoir writes, "The truth is that for man she is an amusement, a pleasure, company, an inessential boon; he is for her the meaning, the justification of her existence."[11] This is clearly the relationship between Booker and Elizabeth at the beginning of the story: she is delighted with the world, as she has not really seen it before, and Booker finds this amusing, at best. Elizabeth is helpful, or a boon, but not a necessary one, at least not at first. Booker frees her; he gives her a story and a purpose: to go to Paris. Without Booker Elizabeth is nothing, certainly not a person or a character. Because she has to depend on Booker for her existence, she is still not free.

Although Elizabeth's skills as a companion are not essential, she does, later in the game, reveal a very important and necessary skill that drives forward the concluding plotline: opening tears. It is unclear what a tear is. Even Elizabeth, who has lived with them her whole life, doesn't completely understand them, in part because she wasn't ever allowed to fully explore them. As her powers grew, so did the syphon. She does say a number of times that she feels the tears are a form of wish fulfillment and that "Whenever I get anxious, tears have a way of appearing." These tears are completely unique to Elizabeth and are entirely essential to the gameplay. You cannot advance past certain areas without Elizabeth's tears, and they become increasingly necessary as the story progresses.

Despite the growing need for tears, when Booker first sees Elizabeth open one to let a bee out, he is not pleased. She claims that she could use them to help, but his response is that they look like a "short cut to getting us killed." He "can handle what comes along." The tears, then, at first are seen as something frightening, and not helpful to Booker, in particular because he "doesn't really understand" them. Booker's response to Elizabeth and her powers is analogous to men's response to women. Men do not understand because they see women as wholly different and foreign—or, as de Beauvoir puts it, "Other"—and men therefore try to limit or suppress women. Rather than see Elizabeth's difference as a good thing, or perhaps just different, Booker, like other men, sees it as something foreign and unwanted. Elizabeth, because she is so used to accepting what the men in her life demand of her, obliges. It is not until later, not until she is truly emancipated, that she

gains more control over her power and that her power is seen and
used as an essential boon.

"My Days of Victimhood are Done"—Elizabeth

Although Elizabeth spends a great deal of time in cages, she is eventually liberated. De Beauvoir gives us only sparse details of what the
liberation of women looks like because for her "the free woman is just
being born," and her project in *The Second Sex* is mainly the description and explanation of the oppression of women.[12] She does claim a
number of times, though, that it is through economic equality, like
gainful employment, that women can guarantee their freedom.[13]
Gainful employment is not a goal for Elizabeth, yet we can understand de Beauvoir's point by looking at what about employment she
finds to be beneficial to the emancipation of women. In particular, de
Beauvoir argues that a woman can be free "once she ceases to be a
parasite," once she is "productive, active" and once she takes "possession of... and senses her responsibility."[14] She must "be permitted to
take her chances in her own interest and in the interest of all."[15]

Elizabeth's emancipation is not something that comes about all at
once, but rather develops over the course of the game. There are pivotal points of the story in which she does what de Beauvoir requires
of a liberated woman: she becomes more active, brings her own
interest to bear, and becomes responsible. One pivotal point in the
game for Elizabeth occurs when she encounters the ghost of her
mother and a fight ensues. It is only when Elizabeth learns of Lady
Comstock's feelings and circumstances that she begins to see that
Lady Comstock was oppressed by Zachary as well. Elizabeth comments, "All locked up in there. Looks like you and I have some
common ground." As soon as she realizes that her mother suffered a
fate similar to her own, she talks to the ghost and they cease fighting.
Elizabeth and Lady Comstock's union fits de Beauvoir's claim that the
liberation of women must be a "collective one."[16] In order for this
collective freedom to occur, women must stop fighting with each
other for the approval of men. Elizabeth and Lady Comstock must
stop their infighting. They are, after all, both in the situation they are
in due to Zachary. That is where their attention must be turned; that
is where they must take their fight, rather than at each other.

Another pivotal point of the game for Elizabeth comes in an alternate reality. We see glimpses of an aged Elizabeth who fulfills her father's prophecy by setting New York City ablaze. We hear her over Columbia's loudspeaker mimicking Zachary's words and ideals. She, the aged Elizabeth, is what can happen under the oppression of men. As de Beauvoir writes, "To see things clearly is not her business, for she has been taught to accept masculine authority. So she gives up criticizing, judging for herself, and leaves all this to the superior caste."[17] Elizabeth gives up her questioning and her responsibility to become what Zachary wants her to be. Old Elizabeth seems all too aware of her oppressed position, hauntingly remarking: "What would happen if I took off the leash and found I was as obedient as ever?" This quote speaks volumes, because it reinforces the idea that even outside of a literal cage, one can still be caged, and because it echoes the situation of oppressed women as leashed but accepting of the leash; or, as de Beauvoir puts it, consenting to their own oppression.

This aged Elizabeth is important not only because she shows us what can happen under the oppressive thumb of men, but also because of her assistance to young Elizabeth. In particular, old Elizabeth gives a note to Booker to give to the young Elizabeth. This note contains information essential to Elizabeth's liberation: how to control her warden Songbird. Old Elizabeth's actions help to free young Elizabeth and reveal another collective of women working together toward their mutual freedom.

In these examples we can perceive a few common themes. Elizabeth sees with greater clarity the world around her; in particular, she sees the wires of the cages working together to form a system of dominance. Further, she sees that Zachary Comstock is responsible for all of these wires. Additionally, in these instances we see Elizabeth take action and responsibility. It is she, and not Booker, who leads each of these quest lines and who figures out the next step in the journey and acts. Elizabeth no longer wholly relies on Booker for her answers, but seeks them herself. None of this is to say that Elizabeth achieved her freedom on her own, or that these are the only instances of her learning and acting. Booker is very important to her freedom, but he is not sufficient for it. Rather, as de Beauvoir claims, in order for woman to truly be free, she must end her total dependence on men and act for herself.

Elizabeth's journey to freedom is not without strife. Her father, obviously, wants her back in the cage and the citizens of Columbia are constantly trying to recapture her. Not only does she struggle for freedom with the citizens of Columbia, but also with her companion Booker. We first see this conflict when Elizabeth apprehends that Booker is not being honest with her. After helping him get to the airship for their goal of going to Paris, she realizes, when she looks at the longitude and latitude of their destination, that they are in fact going to New York. When Elizabeth realizes Booker's deceit, she knocks him out and runs away. Eventually they are reunited, though her attitude is certainly changed. She reverts to calling him Mr. DeWitt and tells him, "Don't get too comfortable with my company, Mr. DeWitt. You are a means to an end." Booker responds to her aggression in like kind, at one point rather gruffly saying to her, "My busting you out; what do you think that was? Charity?" This tension between the two is entirely necessary. After all, Booker has been benefiting from Elizabeth's submission for most of the game. It is also a natural conclusion of Elizabeth, or any woman, struggling against oppression. As de Beauvoir writes, "He is very well pleased to remain the sovereign subject, the absolute supreme, the essential being; he refuses to accept his companion as an equal in any concrete way. She replies to his lack of confidence by assuming an aggressive attitude."[18] This quarrel will continue, de Beauvoir argues, "as long as men and women fail to recognize each other as peers."[19] In the beginning, Booker sees Elizabeth as a means to an end. As she gains more freedom, she does the same to him. It is not until the two see each other as equals that this tension ends and that she is closer to real freedom.

"Smother Him in the Crib" — Booker

The liberation of Elizabeth is a necessary and important part of the story of Columbia. As mentioned before, there is a link between Elizabeth's increasing freedom and her centrality to the story. As she begins to stick up for herself, questioning Booker's motivation and activities, she becomes more necessary to Booker and the game. Her tears, which Booker at first scorned, are now necessary to move the plot along: you must open tears to bring the tools to the warehouse and save Lin, for example. Elizabeth, as liberated, then transitions from being an object to a subject as the game goes on. She is no longer an inessential companion, but a very necessary and integral part of the game. Her ability to help increases, as does the need for it. Her skills are now seen as equal to Booker's shooting prowess. Rather than Booker being the one in charge, the most powerful and necessary one, they become equals. He needs her tears, help, and direction, and she becomes more active, more involved, and less dependent on him.

Not only are Elizabeth's skills more and more useful as she becomes more and more free, but she also, in a sense, becomes the protagonist of the story. While obviously you, as the player, do not get to control her, her actions and desires become the driving force for the conclusion of the game. It is Elizabeth, and not Booker, who wants to see her mother. It is she, and not Booker, who wants to go to Comstock and confront him (Booker is the one who wants to go to Paris now!). It is also Elizabeth, more so than Booker, who drives us toward the game's ending.

Elizabeth is the one who figures out the ending long before Booker; she is able to see it all, while he remains confused. Elizabeth explains that despite the fact that they killed Comstock in their universe, there are still millions of other universes where Comstock lives. Booker then states that they must smother Comstock in his cradle so that there will never be a Comstock in any universe at any time. As far as video games are concerned, this is as close as we get to the final boss: we must kill Comstock in his cradle and only then will we have won the game. We are stunned to learn that Booker is Comstock and has become Comstock through a baptism. A number of Elizabeths come to the baptism and drown Booker/Comstock, thereby defeating the final boss. What we might have expected is for Booker to save the day, while Elizabeth stands idly by (à la Princess Peach), yet she is in fact very active and takes part in the final boss kill. It is not Elizabeth alone who does this deed, though. She does not kill Booker against his will. Such a reading of the ending might lead one to the false conclusion that the liberation of women automatically means the destruction of men. Rather, Booker knows that this must happen and goes into the water willingly. The death of the final boss is something that the two undertake as equals, both active, both involved, and both pursuing their interests. This final act, done together, allows absolute freedom for both: Booker's debt is wiped away, and Elizabeth will never again be subjected to her tower.[20]

Notes

1. Simone de Beauvoir, *The Ethics of Ambiguity*, trans. Bernard Frechtman (New York: Citadel Press, 1976), 37.
2. Simone de Beauvoir, *The Second Sex*, trans. H.M. Parshley (New York: Everyman's Library, 1993), 629.
3. De Beauvoir, *Ethics of Ambiguity*, 38.
4. Marilyn Frye, "Oppression," in *Gender Basics: Feminist Perspectives on Women and Men*, ed. Ann Minas (Belmont, CA: Wadsworth, 2000), 12.
5. Ibid.
6. De Beauvoir, *Second Sex*, xliii.
7. Ibid., 756.
8. Ibid., xliii.
9. Ibid., 758.
10. Ibid., 724.
11. Ibid., 758.
12. Ibid., 750.
13. Ibid., 660 and 713.
14. Ibid., 713.
15. Ibid., 750.
16. Ibid., 660.
17. Ibid., 631.
18. Ibid., 753.
19. Ibid., 754.
20. A special thanks to Matthew Ross for the helpful insights.

Part II
TEARS, TIME, AND REALITY

Rapture in a Physical World
Did Andrew Ryan Choose the Impossible?

James Cook

In Rapture some mad shit happens: there are Plasmids that allow players to fire bees (yes, that's right, bees!) out of their hands, generate electricity bolts, set enemies on fire, pick stuff up using telekinetic powers, and much more. We also see the "ghosts of Rapture" as a result of our use of ADAM. Someone might say that in the Rapture world, physicalism—the view that everything in the world is physical, or rather, depends on the physical—is false. They might say that we need to bring in separate categories of existence to adequately explain entities like ghosts. So, in this case, if physicalism is true, Andrew Ryan really did *choose the impossible* when he built Rapture. Or did he?

Physicalism, Ryan's Putter, and Ghosts

What is physicalism? Physicalism is the view that everything is physical, as opposed to dualism, which is the view that some things are physical and some things are non-physical. This is not an incredibly helpful answer, though, because it doesn't tell us what it takes to be a physical thing and what it takes to be a non-physical thing. We can attribute some properties to physical things, such as being located in space and time, and being able to cause physical events (whatever *physical* events may be). But this is not enough. Luckily, there are a couple of theories concerning what counts as physical and what

BioShock and Philosophy: Irrational Game, Rational Book, First Edition. Edited by Luke Cuddy.
© 2015 John Wiley & Sons, Inc. Published 2015 by John Wiley & Sons, Inc.

doesn't. One theory is that physical things are those that can be completely described by the vocabulary of the best possible theory of physics (presumably this would be a complete physics). Physicalism would thus be the view that this theory of physics would completely specify all the fundamental categories, all the ingredients we need to make the world. Another theory is that the physical properties are the ones needed to account for the objects we accept as physical; for example, Andrew Ryan's putter.[1] The physicalist's claim would be that these properties are the only ones we need to account for the rest of the world. So the same basic ingredients we need to make Ryan's putter (the physical properties) can be used to account for weird stuff like Plasmids and ghosts.

If we go for the first option and hold that physical properties are the ones that a complete theory of physics would specify, then one issue we would have to deal with is that the *BioShock* world may have a different complete theory of physics. Objects move around differently in the game than they would in the actual world (because of the physics engine and whatnot). So we would have to heavily revise our theories of physics in order to account for a world that works the same way as a game's physics engine. If this is so, then we may not be able to identify the physical properties with the properties that the best possible theory of physics mentions. The best theory of physics would differ between our world and the *BioShock* world. So there wouldn't be one class of "physical" properties that the physicalist would say existed.

This is not quite right, however. In worlds with physics much like the *BioShock* world's physics we could still tell the difference between the physical things and the non-physical things. The physical things would just be the things mentioned by the best possible theory of physics in that world. What counts as physical may differ from world to world, but there are some things that we would not consider physical in any situation. Beings made out of ectoplasm (if you haven't seen *Ghostbusters*, it might still be on Netflix, depending when you're reading this) and angels would be excluded from a mature theory of physics.

The second option—where the basic ingredients needed to account for obviously physical objects can be used to account for ghosts and weird stuff—may not be the best for our purposes. The ghosts, the Plasmids, and the Little Sisters in Rapture may be made out of completely different ingredients to the things in the actual world. Perhaps ADAM could not be realized with the kind of stuff (chemicals and so on) we have in the actual world, and so then the stuff in Rapture would be radically unlike the stuff we have here.

Plasmids and Ghosts in a Physical World

Now we come to the problem of fitting the Plasmids and the ghosts into the physical world.

Plasmids

Plasmids give the people who use them fantastical abilities. With Plasmids one has the capacity to set things on fire, create mini-tornados, hypnotize enemies, shoot electro-bolts, and other crazy stuff—though for the sake of ease we'll focus on the "incinerate" Plasmid. Why couldn't these be physically realizable? Again, without any principled scientific reason for not being able to genetically modify someone so that they can set things alight, we would be back to the view that this is too weird to be physically possible. It would have to be some form of magic.

It's true, humans cannot shoot fire out of their hands in the actual world (sorry, psychics). They just cannot generate the kind of energy required to do this. It would be physically impossible for a human being with our biology to demonstrate pyrokinesis. But remember, in *BioShock* we are not talking about normal human subjects. We are talking about genetically modified humans. *If* a human's biology was changed in some drastic way, then perhaps it would be physically possible to generate fire. This seems to be what happens in Rapture. Brigid Tenenbaum and others pioneered the production of Plasmids with ADAM, which is taken from sea slugs. The inhabitants of Rapture had to change their genetic make-up with ADAM before they could gain pyrokinesis. This means that the impossibility of non-genetically modified humans performing pyrokinesis does not entail the impossibility of Splicers doing so. However, could all this be told in a physical vocabulary? If ADAM is a magical property, then presumably it cannot. I could not say for sure that the story about the ADAM-fueled genetic modifications can be told in a physical vocabulary, but there are a few reasons for thinking that it could be.

Genetic modification is physically possible, as is the production of fire (along with pretty much all of the results of the Plasmids). So while it may be pretty much impossible for any scientist to do in the actual world (we don't have the luxury of ADAM), it may be a very distant possibility. And bear in mind what the fundamental physical vocabulary would consist in: it would be the language of electrons, quarks, and the like (or maybe the equivalent in the best theory of physics). There wouldn't be any problem in principle of accounting for these goings-on in this physical language—aside from the fact that it would be really hard to do. We can't even describe special sciences in a completely physical vocabulary, but this doesn't mean that one couldn't do so in principle.

Ghosts

Another potential problem for the physicalist are the ghosts of Rapture. The existence of ghosts would seem to disprove physicalism, because ghosts are composed of ectoplasm and ectoplasm could not be described in a physical vocabulary. This may have been the thinking of a student whose essay a friend of mine marked. The essay boiled down to: "My Nan saw a ghost once; therefore dualism is true." Now, obviously this is not a good argument. The main problem is that even if the Nan was sincere she could have easily been hallucinating, and so she is not the best source of evidence. However, it raises the question of whether we would have to bring in extra categories of existence, besides the physical, to account for ghosts. As stated, if the ghosts are made out of some kind of ectoplasm, then yes, it is very likely that we would. However, the ghosts of Rapture may be a different case. In an audio recording, which is one of our only sources of information about the ghosts, general contractor Bill McDonough says:

> Seems like some poor blighters have started seeing ghosts. Ghosts! Ryan tells me it's a side effect of this Plasmid business. One poor sod's memories getting passed on to another through genetic sampling. Leaks. Lunatics. Rebellion. And now bleeding ghosts. Ain't life in Rapture grand?

So what do we know about ghosts from this quote and from our own in-game experience of them?

- They are leftover memories of Splicers.
- They are a result of excessive use of Plasmids.
- You cannot interact with them.
- When you see the ghosts your whole visual field goes dim and static.

These ghosts don't cause any problem for physicalism because they exist in virtue of gene-swapping and ADAM. Presumably genes are physical, and, as we have established, ADAM seems to be describable in physical terms. If these memories are constituted by transferred genes, and those genes are physical, then the ghosts are also physical. This view is similar to what is called "supervenience physicalism," which is the view that everything that exists is physical or supervenes on the physical. Supervenience here means that one set of facts depends on another set of facts. As the Australian philosopher David Chalmers puts it: "B-properties supervene on A-properties if no two possible situations are identical with respect to their A-properties while differing in their B-properties."[2] In this way, a very rough characterization of supervenience physicalism would be the view that no two possible situations are different with respect to any properties if they do not differ in their physical properties.

If it is correct that facts about the ghosts of Rapture supervene on the physical facts, then physicalism would be preserved. That we could do this is not such a radical claim if we accept that facts about our biology and facts about ADAM are physical facts. So ghosts cause no problem for physicalism if the following principle holds:

- The facts about the ghosts of Rapture supervene on the physical facts if no two possible situations are identical with respect to the physical facts while differing in the facts about ghosts.

We could also posit a similar principle for all the other crazy stuff that happens in Rapture. For example:

- The facts concerning Plasmids supervene on the physical facts if no two possible situations are identical with respect to the physical facts while differing in the facts about Plasmids.

Of course, we would have to give good reasons for positing these principles, which I think we have.

The Smell of Poo and Ghosts

Many of the classic arguments against physicalism also try to show that a physicalist worldview cannot completely account for certain subject matter. For example, there are quite a few arguments that purport to show that mental facts don't depend on physical facts. Most of these are based around the qualitative feel that we have when in some mental states. Take Chalmers' zombie argument, according to which it would be possible for two beings to be physically identical and yet for one to have consciousness while the other lacks consciousness. If this is right, then consciousness does not supervene on the physical facts and this form of physicalism is false.[3] The reason for accepting Chalmers' argument is basically that there is a qualitative gap between the physical facts and the mental facts (I won't explain the whole argument here). The way in which some philosophers have interpreted the problem with accounting for consciousness with a purely physical description of the world is by suggesting that physical facts are objective while facts about our sensations—like the smell of poo—are subjective.[4]

There seems to be no qualitative gap in the same way for the spooky stuff in Rapture, however. There would not be any extra subjective information we could give for an explanation in objective terms that would add anything substantial to our description of telekinesis or ghosts; we could completely describe these phenomena in objective terms.

The Last Bit

The world of Rapture, though very different from the actual world, poses no unique problem for physicalism. Part of the reason for thinking that Rapture is not physically realizable is that the technology is so far advanced that it looks magical. But recall science fiction author Arthur C. Clarke's third law, suggesting that any sufficiently advanced technology is indistinguishable from magic. Less technologically advanced cultures would perhaps view modern technology as spooky stuff in the same way as we view the technology of Rapture. Our technology turned out to be physically realizable—perhaps Rapture's is too.

Notes

1. A view rather like this is found in Frank Jackson, *From Metaphysics to Ethics: A Defence of Conceptual Analysis* (Oxford: Clarendon Press, 1998). Also check out the *Stanford Encyclopedia of Philosophy* entry on physicalism, http://plato.stanford.edu/entries/physicalism/.

2. David Chalmers, *The Conscious Mind: In Search of a Fundamental Theory* (New York: Oxford University Press, 1996), 33.
3. Ibid., 93–99.
4. Thomas Nagel holds that we cannot give an explanation of the qualia of our sensations—their "what-it-is-likeness"—in terms of objective facts (these would presumably include physical facts), as those objective facts would be consistent with the absence of qualia, or rather the "what-it-is-likeness" of experiences. See Thomas Nagel, "What Is It Like to Be a Bat?" *Philosophical Review* 83 (1974): 435–450.

6

Would You Kindly Bring Us the Girl and Wipe Away the Debt

Free Will and Moral Responsibility in *BioShock Infinite*

Oliver Laas

"Father" Zachary Hale Comstock is a self-professed prophet, religious zealot, and racist, who has kept his "heir" under lock and key in the floating city of Columbia. This inheritor is a young woman, Elizabeth, who has the ability to open "tears" or "doorways" into alternate worlds and different times. Comstock subjects her to his will, ultimately leading her to destroy New York in 1984 to fulfill his "prophecy." Clearly, Comstock is morally responsible for his actions.

Booker DeWitt is a washed-up, disgraced ex-Pinkerton agent haunted by his participation in the Wounded Knee Massacre. He enters Columbia to rescue Elizabeth in exchange for having his gambling debts settled. After much bloodshed, Booker saves Elizabeth and kills Comstock. Certainly, Booker is blameworthy for the carnage, and praiseworthy for saving Elizabeth.

But (spoiler alert) Booker *is* Comstock. In the past, Booker attended a baptism to assuage his guilt over Wounded Knee. In some worlds he rejected the baptism, got married, had a daughter, Anna, and ended up as an indebted alcoholic ex-Pinkerton agent. In other worlds he accepted the baptism, took the name Zachary Hale Comstock, founded Columbia, and acquired his "heir" by opening

BioShock and Philosophy: Irrational Game, Rational Book, First Edition. Edited by Luke Cuddy.
© 2015 John Wiley & Sons, Inc. Published 2015 by John Wiley & Sons, Inc.

a tear to the Booker world and buying Anna in exchange for wiping away Booker's debts. In the Comstock world, Anna is renamed Elizabeth in order to conceal her true origins. Who is responsible for what? According to common sense, both Booker and Comstock are responsible for their own actions. Yet the game's ending implies otherwise.

"Liberty Means Responsibility" — George Bernard Shaw

Questions of responsibility are intimately related to the free will problem—a perennial issue in philosophy that has at least two aspects.

The first aspect concerns the kind of freedom that can generally be defined as the ability to act without external or internal constraints. This differs from *surface freedoms*, such as the freedom to travel anywhere or to buy anything one likes. The relevant deeper sense of freedom is supposedly captured by the notion of "free will."[1]

The second aspect involves moral and legal responsibility. Free will is related to notions of accountability, blameworthiness, and praiseworthiness. For example, in *BioShock*, Jack (or the player) can do one of two things to the Little Sisters: he can either harvest them—this yields more ADAM for enhancing his abilities, but kills the girls—or cure them—this yields less ADAM, but saves the girls. Suppose that Jack harvests one of the Little Sisters. We would say that Jack is blameworthy for what he did because he could have chosen otherwise. However, suppose that someone puts a gun to Jack's head and orders him to cure the girl or forfeit his life; Jack rationally chooses the former. Despite the good deed, we would not praise him since he could not have reasonably chosen otherwise.

This example rests on two commonsensical intuitions. The first intuition is: "People should be held responsible for their actions unless there are exonerating circumstances." The second intuition says: "Circumstances in which people are unable to act freely are exonerating."[2] The latter can also be called the *Principle of Alternate Possibilities* (PAP): a person is morally responsible for what he or she has done only if he or she could have done otherwise.[3] PAP is generally accepted in philosophy, everyday deliberation, and legal reasoning.

"No Animal is Born Free..."—Zachary Hale Comstock

Determinism has been known in many guises throughout history, but William James (1842–1910) describes the underlying intuition lucidly:

> [Determinism] professes that those parts of the universe already laid down absolutely appoint and decree what the other parts shall be. The future has no ambiguous possibilities hidden in its womb: the part we call the present is compatible with only one totality. Any other future complement than the one fixed from eternity is impossible.[4]

Determinism is a kind of conditional necessity: if the antecedent determining condition occurs, then so does the consequent condition. If some form of determinism is true, then PAP is false. And without PAP there seems to be no moral responsibility either.

The contrary to determinism is indeterminism, which claims that some events simply occur without determining causes or prior conditions. Such happenings are often characterized in terms of chance, uncertainty, or randomness.

Between the Confines of Necessity and Free Will

In philosophy there are two different standpoints on the free will problem: compatibilism argues that free will and determinism are not mutually exclusive; incompatibilism claims that free will and determinism are mutually exclusive.

Compatibilists rely on two additional commonsense intuitions about determinism and free will. The third intuition is: "Discoveries in physics and the life sciences indicate that determinism applies to people as well as inanimate particles, but this does not undermine ascriptions of moral responsibility." And the fourth intuition concerns the nature of freedom, namely: "Freedom is the absence of compulsion, coercion, or constraint."[5] Compatibilists wish to maintain all four commonsense intuitions along with the scientific worldview.[6] Influential philosophers like Thomas Hobbes (1588–1679), John Locke (1632–1704), David Hume (1711–76), and John Stuart Mill (1806–73) have been compatibilists.

Incompatibilists reject the third intuition while maintaining the others. Their position could be summed up by this maxim: "There is no determinism—man is free, man is freedom."[7]

Measurements in Different Worlds

The question of Booker's responsibility depends on whether the world is deterministic or indeterministic, and whether one is a compatibilist or an incompatibilist.

Classical physics postulated that the universe changes over time according to definite and unequivocal physical laws, so that its state at any time is completely determined by its state at prior times and the physical laws of nature. This leaves little room for incompatibilist free will. Quantum mechanics, on the other hand, seems to imply that the world is indeterministic.[8]

BioShock Infinite paints a metaphysical picture that treats the *many-worlds interpretation of quantum mechanics* as reality. This view was originally proposed by the physicist Hugh Everett III (1930–82)[9] as an answer to the measurement problem in quantum mechanics, and as a way of avoiding indeterminacy.

The crux of the problem is this.[10] According to quantum mechanics, each observable physical system—anything from a particle to a person—has wavelike properties, and their evolution in time is represented formally by a wave function. At one point in the game, it is crucial for Booker and Elizabeth to determine whether the imprisoned Chen Lin is alive. Suppose that in the cell with him is a device consisting of a Geiger counter, a small amount of a radioactive substance, a hammer, and a flask of poison. In the course of one hour, an atom of the substance either decays or not. If it does, the Geiger counter goes off, triggers the hammer, which shatters the flask and kills Chen Lin. The wave function of this system—composed of Chen Lin, the device, and the cell—is interpreted statistically. This means that prior to observation, Booker and Elizabeth only have a certain probability of finding Chen Lin alive. According to the traditional Copenhagen Interpretation of quantum mechanics, one would say that prior to observation it is objectively indeterminate whether Chen Lin is dead or not—he is both dead and alive. Yet when Booker and Elizabeth open the cell door, Chen Lin will be either dead or alive. The discrepancy is explained by the collapse postulate: by observing Chen Lin, Booker and Elizabeth compel the wave function to "collapse" to a determinate state, and assign to Chen Lin either the property of being alive or the property of being dead. It seems to follow that whether Chen Lin is alive or not depends somehow on observation.[11]

The many-worlds interpretation proposes that the wave function never collapses. Instead, the universe literally "branches" into two or more different, non-interacting but equally real worlds, each of which corresponds to a definite possible measurement. With every observation the world is continually split into an astonishing number of branches.[12] The upshot is that "all possible outcomes [of an observed event] occur; each one is the point of departure for other forkings."[13] Hence, the universe is really a *multiverse*, a set of possible parallel universes or worlds, all of which have more or less different histories[14] that together "embrace all possibilities of time."[15] As a result, indeterminacy and observer participation are denied,[16] because everything in the multiverse is determined, and all worlds obey deterministic physical laws.[17] Since PAP does not hold in *BioShock Infinite*'s multiverse, Booker is not responsible for his actions, says the incompatibilist. But does responsibility require PAP?

Would You Kindly?

The contemporary philosopher Harry Frankfurt has presented an influential argument for compatibilism by claiming that there is no link between moral responsibility and PAP.[18] The illustrations involved in his claims have subsequently become known as "Frankfurt-type examples." These usually involve some constraint that does not play a role in the agent's choices or behavior, but nonetheless renders that behavior inevitable.[19]

As Jack exits the bathysphere, when he first sets foot in Rapture, he is contacted by a man named Atlas (the game's main antagonist, Frank Fontaine, in disguise), who guides him through the ruins of the city and has him perform various tasks. Atlas's instructions often involve the phrase "would you kindly" that, unbeknownst to Jack, is a programmed trigger phrase for controlling his actions. Suppose that Jack is faced with the choice of either harvesting or curing a Little Sister. Atlas wants him to harvest the girl and, due to the trigger phrase, he can ensure that Jack complies. However, in order not to tip his hand, Atlas only interferes if Jack shows a prior sign that he is going to choose to cure the girl.[20] But suppose that Jack chooses to harvest the Little Sister. He thereby does what Atlas wanted without any need for intervention. It follows that Jack acted without compulsion, and is therefore morally responsible for harvesting the girl. Yet he also could not have done otherwise.

Frankfurt-type examples are designed to show that an agent is morally responsible even if PAP does not hold.

BioShock Infinite as a Frankfurt-type Example

BioShock Infinite can be interpreted as a Frankfurt-style example on the level of both its structure and its narrative content.

The structure of modern first-person shooters (FPS), such as *BioShock Infinite*, is characterized by constants—narrative points with predetermined outcomes connected by a small number of forking paths—and variables—the players' restricted freedom in navigating the game's constants. Player actions are confined to realizing one out of a limited number of prescribed outcomes.[21] The game's structure acts as a constraint for the player, letting him act with little to no meaningful possibility to do otherwise.

BioShock Infinite's plot is intimately tied to the game's structure, so much so that it could be treated as a metaphor for the latter. Booker's relationship with the Comstock world is similar to the player's relationship with the game's structure. The plot's constants, like the coin toss always coming out heads, indicate that the Luteces have brought numerous Bookers into the Comstock world before. The variables that are there—choosing Elizabeth's necklace or deciding Slate's fate—have no effect on the game's outcome. Each Booker introduced into the Comstock world is a foreign element caught in a reality that does not originally involve him, and precludes him from doing otherwise than set by that world's established history.

Thus, if Frankfurt is right and if compatibilism is correct, Booker is morally responsible. However, the game's ending seems to imply an even stronger thesis about responsibility.

"We All Make Choices, But in the End Our Choices Make Us"—Andrew Ryan

To redeem himself, Booker must never make the choice of accepting the baptism in the first place. Moreover, every Booker in every sufficiently similar world must either renounce the baptism or never make the choice at all. To ensure that no Booker in the multiverse ever makes the choice, every Elizabeth and every Booker travel back in time to a moment before the baptism, and every Elizabeth drowns every Booker. This can be interpreted in at least two ways: (1) every Elizabeth kills every Booker in the multiverse at baptism, or (2) every Elizabeth kills only those Bookers in the multiverse who accepted the baptism. Let's concentrate on (1), since it is the more interesting case.

Intuitively, it seems that each individual in the multiverse is responsible for what they have done in their world, since worlds are spatio-temporally and causally isolated. *BioShock Infinite* suggests that moral responsibility is not world-bound. Why else would a Booker, who renounced the baptism in the past, still be accountable, and end up being drowned? The reason could be that identity is a necessary condition for ascribing responsibility. To hold someone accountable for something after the fact requires that they be the same person they were while committing the act. Booker has multiple counterparts across the multiverse. Which one of them is he? In a sense, he is all of them. As the universe splits at each observation, so do the observers.[22] The proper name "Booker DeWitt" when uttered within a world refers to the name's bearer in that world. But from a hypothetical multiverse perspective, "Booker DeWitt" refers to all individuals bearing that name in all alternate worlds.

BioShock Infinite's ending implies that responsibility is ascribed to an individual from a multiverse perspective. From this, it follows that there is mutual responsibility between all counterparts in the multiverse, since they are all parts of a transworld individual—each Booker DeWitt in some world is a part of the Booker DeWitt that exists across all worlds and all times. Call this the *thesis of transworld moral responsibility*. Not only is every Booker responsible for the actions of every other, it is also impossible for any Booker to redeem himself.

The Impossible Price of Clemency

The price of clemency in *BioShock Infinite* is paradoxical, since every Elizabeth travels back in time before she was born to kill her father. This is a variant of the *grandfather paradox*, which has been taken to show that time travel is impossible, because it implies a break in the causal chain that links the time traveler with his father.

Backward time travel within the many-worlds framework takes the time traveler to a different branch of history than the one he departed from. When he kills his grandfather, the act takes place in, or results in the creation of, an alternate world where the traveler's counterpart did not exist. The original world, from which the traveler departed, however, remains unaltered.[23] The upshot is that restitution for Booker is impossible, since each time an Elizabeth kills a Booker in the past, the universe simply branches, leaving the original world's timeline intact—nothing changes.

"One Can't Believe Impossible Things"[24]

BioShock Infinite has a rather stark stance on moral responsibility. First, one is morally responsible even if one could not have done otherwise. Second, from the fact that responsibility is attributed from a hypothetical multiverse perspective, two things follow: moral principles are not relative to worlds (moral relativism), but are the same in all of them (moral objectivism); and, as a corollary, one is responsible for one's own deeds as well as those of one's counterparts in the multiverse. Third, the past cannot be altered, and choices cannot be unmade. The upshot is that we are all inescapably blameworthy for something, because either we or one of our counterparts somewhere in the multiverse have done, are doing, or will do something blameworthy. This can be seen as a secular version of the Christian doctrine of original sin,[25] especially when interpreted as resulting in the human race being comprised of a *massa damnata*,[26] a condemned mass. Another shared feature with religious doctrines is *BioShock Infinite*'s objective view of moral principles as being the same in all worlds.

To my knowledge, the possibility of transworld moral responsibility has not been explicitly proposed in the philosophical literature.[27] This is understandable—the thesis seems incredible because it assigns praise or blame unreasonably and unfairly. Suppose that there are two worlds, w_1 and w_2, identical except that in w_1 Jack$_1$ harvests all the Little Sisters he meets, whereas in w_2 Jack$_2$ cures all the Little Sisters he runs into. If transworld moral responsibility is true, then Jack$_1$ should receive praise whenever Jack$_2$ saves a Little Sister. But intuitively this seems wrong: Jack$_1$ should not receive praise for something he did not do nor had the chance to influence. Likewise, $Jack_2$ should not be blamed each time $Jack_1$ harvests a Little Sister.

One reason for not taking the idea of transworld responsibility seriously is that it conflicts with the generally accepted maxim of "ought implies can";[28] that is, if an agent ought to do X, then it is possible for him to do X.[29] There is a connection between its being the case that an agent ought to do X, and the agent's being blameworthy for not doing X. But there could be cases in which an agent is blameworthy for X-ing or not X-ing, but in fact cannot X. To expect in such situations that an agent should or should not have done something that he or she really cannot do is to expect him or her to have done the impossible. Because $Jack_2$ cannot influence the actions of any of his counterparts in other worlds, it would be unfair and unreasonable to consider him blameworthy or responsible for their actions. Indeed, what should he have done?[30]

In response, one could try to challenge the intuition summarized in the "ought implies can" maxim or argue for moral relativism. However, in this world our philosophical adventure has come to an end. We will not pursue the plausibility of transworld responsibility further. My mission has simply been to show that *BioShock Infinite* raises intriguing questions about free will and offers possibilities for contemplation. The rest is up to you.

Notes

1. Robert Kane, *A Contemporary Introduction to Free Will* (Oxford: Oxford University Press, 2005), 2.
2. John Earman, *A Primer on Determinism* (Dordrecht: D. Reidel, 1986), 236.
3. Harry G. Frankfurt, "Alternate Possibilities and Moral Responsibility," in *The Importance of What We Care About: Philosophical Essays* (Cambridge: Cambridge University Press, 1988), 1.
4. William James, "The Dilemma of Determinism," in *William James: Writings 1878–1899* (New York: Library of America, 1992), 569–570.
5. See Earman, *Primer on Determinism*, 236, 237.
6. Kane, *Contemporary Introduction to Free Will*, 12–13.
7. Jean-Paul Sartre, *Existentialism Is a Humanism*, trans. Carol Macomber (New Haven, CT: Yale University Press, 2007), 29.

8. David Hodgson, "Quantum Physics, Consciousness, and Free Will," in *The Oxford Handbook of Free Will*, ed. Robert Kane (Oxford: Oxford University Press, 2002), 85–86.

9. Everett's original proposal can be found in Hugh Everett, "Relative State Formulation of Quantum Mechanics," in *The Many-Worlds Interpretation of Quantum Mechanics*, eds. Bryce S. De Witt & Neill Graham (Princeton, NJ: Princeton University Press, 1973), 141–150.

10. What follows is based on Erwin Schrödinger's (1887–1961) famous cat paradox, which was intended to show some of the counter-intuitive results that follow from the Copenhagen Interpretation of quantum mechanics.

11. For additional details see Max Jammer, *The Philosophy of Quantum Mechanics: The Interpretations of Quantum Mechanics in Historical Perspective* (New York: John Wiley & Sons, 1974); Bernard D'Espagnat, *Conceptual Foundations of Quantum Mechanics*, 2nd edn (Reading, MA: Perseus Books, 1999); David J. Griffiths, *Introduction to Quantum Mechanics* (Upper Saddle River, NJ: Prentice Hall, 1995).

12. Earman, *Primer on Determinism*, 224; Jammer, *Philosophy of Quantum Mechanics*, 507–508, 512–513.

13. Jorge Luis Borges, "The Garden of Forking Paths," in *Labyrinths: Selected Stories and Other Writings*, eds. Donald A. Yates & James E. Irby (New York: New Directions, 1964), 40.

14. David Deutsch, *The Fabric of Reality: The Science of Parallel Universes—and Its Implications* (London: Penguin, 1997), 50–51, 274–276.

15. Borges, "Garden of Forking Paths," 42.

16. Hodgson, "Quantum Physics," 94, 95–96.

17. Deutsch, *Fabric of Reality*, 284.

18. Frankfurt, "Alternate Possibilities."

19. John Martin Fischer, "Frankfurt-Type Examples and Semi-Compatibilism," in *The Oxford Handbook of Free Will*, ed. Robert Kane (Oxford: Oxford University Press, 2002), 281.

20. David Blumenfeld introduced the idea of a prior sign into Frankfurt-type examples in order to better flesh them out. See David C. Blumenfeld, "The Principle of Alternative Possibilities," *Journal of Philosophy* 68 (1971): 339–345.

21. Rune Klevjer, "La via della pistol a: L'estetica dei first person shooter in single player [The way of the gun: the aesthetic of the single-player First Person Shooter]," in *Doom: Giocare in prima persona*, eds. Matteo Bittanti & Sue Morris (Milan: Costa & Nolan, 2006), http://folk.uib.no/smkrk/docs/wayofthegun.pdf.

22. See Deutsch, *Fabric of Reality*, 278, 279.

23. Ibid., 289–320.

24. Lewis Carroll, *Alice's Adventures in Wonderland, and Through the Looking Glass and What Alice Found There* (London: Macmillan, 1911), 205.

25. See Romans 5:12–21, 1 Corinthians 15:22, Psalm 51:5, in *The Holy Bible*, English Standard Version (Wheaton, IL: Crossway Bibles, 2001).

26. This interpretation was put forth by Saint Augustine of Hippo (354–430). See Saint Augustine, *The City of God*, Book XXI, Ch. 12, in *The Works of Aurelius Augustine, Bishop of Hippo*, ed. Marcus Dods, vol. 2 (Edinburgh: T. & T. Clark, 1871).

27. Alvin Plantinga has discussed what he calls *transworld depravity*. Central to the idea is that if a person suffers from transworld depravity, then it was not in God's power to actualize any world in which that person is significantly free and produces moral good but no moral evil. See Alvin Plantinga, *God, Freedom, and Evil* (Grand Rapids, MI: William B. Eerdmans, 1977), 48.

28. This maxim is attributed to Immanuel Kant (1724–1804).

29. See Immanuel Kant, *Critique of Pure Reason*, trans. Paul Guyer & Allen W. Wood (Cambridge: Cambridge University Press, 1998), A548/B576.

30. David Wirderker calls this the "What-should-he-have-done defense" against attributing moral responsibility to agents who act in the kinds of situations described by Frankfurt-type examples. If there is no alternative that the agent should have done, then he is not culpable. See David Widerker, "Responsibility and Frankfurt-Type Examples," in *The Oxford Handbook of Free Will*, ed. Robert Kane (Oxford: Oxford University Press, 2002), 329.

BioShock as Plato's Cave

Roger Travis

Everyone misses the point of Plato's cave. What a coincidence, because everyone also misses the point of *BioShock*. Let's start with the latter. The moment your interactivity with the game is revealed as a fake isn't the moment when you kill Andrew Ryan in a cutscene. It's what happens after that. Atlas tells you to abort the self-destruct sequence, and tacks on a "Would you kindly?" (the phrase that you've just realized controls your actions in the game). At that point, you can run around Andrew Ryan's office as much as you want, shoot at the walls, look at stuff, jump up and down, all to your heart's content. So you don't have to obey Atlas, really.

But the self-destruct sequence won't end either in success or in failure, and the game won't proceed, unless you insert the relevant item in the requisite slot. You have the choice of whether to abort the self-destruct sequence or not, but, positioned as it is, that choice has been exposed as meaningless within the basic fabric of the game's mechanics.

It's like when you're a prisoner in Plato's cave—and you are in fact a prisoner in Plato's cave, take my word for it. It's like when you think you're getting up, and you think you're going outside, and you think you're seeing this thing called the sun.

BioShock and Philosophy: Irrational Game, Rational Book, First Edition. Edited by Luke Cuddy.
© 2015 John Wiley & Sons, Inc. Published 2015 by John Wiley & Sons, Inc.

Is Outside the Cave Real Either?

Let's back up a second and talk cave. Socrates, in *Republic* 7: here's a story about education and non-education. There are these people, chained to seats in a cave, looking at the wall, and on the wall they're watching a shadow-puppet play. They can't get up, they can't turn their heads: this is their universe, this shadow show. They have contests to decide who gets stuff: if you can name what shadow is coming next, you win. Somehow, one of the prisoners gets freed and is forced to go up into the sunlight; it's painful, but he figures out what's going on, and he comes back down and tries to get the others to stand up.

That's when the real trouble starts, though, because none of it's real, because reality is created by the world down below. When you go down, and you try to persuade your fellow prisoners that they have to get up and come with you and go see this amazing thing you found outside, it doesn't go so well. First you try to play their games, the ones where they name which shadow on the wall is coming first, and which second, and get the prizes. (You know, the stuff you get in the "real" world: money, power, gift cards to Amazon.) You think, presumably, that if you can get some of the prizes, the people will listen to you, and they'll come share your amazing discovery.

Unfortunately, though, your eyes are having trouble getting adjusted to the light, and, well, you get owned. Then you get mad. You say, "These games are stupid. Everyone needs to stop right now. It's not real!"

And they kill you.

BioShock Is Better

Actually, *BioShock* does it better, because instead of killing, there's just blah. Blah is running around Andrew Ryan's office, hearing Atlas say, every so often, "Would you kindly abort the self-destruct sequence?"

It would be one thing if the self-destruct sequence actually completed on its own if you didn't abort it. That would be yet another fake meaningful choice in a game universe. The choice means life and death. It would be a little more like Plato's cave, but it would also mean that there was no point: the idea that, as Andrew Ryan himself says, "A man chooses; a slave obeys" would remain, if not intact, at least plausible. You have heroically decided to take a stand for your free will, and you will go down with the, er, town, your rights as a free human individual remaining.

But the genius of *BioShock* is that the possibility space of the game doesn't give that possibility. The rule set of the game says that as a player entering into a fictional universe in which your decisions and manipulations of the gamepad determine some part of the course of the performance of the narrative, you may not fail to abort the self-destruct sequence, as implausibly stretched out as the time taken up by the self-destruct's achievement may become.

The narrative that comprises the universe, and the universe that comprises the narrative—both must have the sequence aborted as an ineluctable feature. Every game creates its possibility space by fore-closing certain choices; that function of rule sets lies at the base of designer Sid Meier's famous definition of a game as a series of interesting choices. Those choices develop their interest precisely because they are available while other choices have been foreclosed. The moment of the self-destruct sequence in *BioShock*, however, is different from most, and precious for its philosophical effect.

It is different and precious because of the way *BioShock* contextualizes it, because of the precise way all the other choices are foreclosed. With the words of Andrew Ryan—"A man chooses; a slave obeys"—ringing in the player's ears, the player, who feels him- or herself to be a man, must obey.

The Other "Choices"

Now we get to confront the two other choices the player does have: leave the game running, but don't disarm the self-destruct; or turn the game off, play a different game, break the console, break the monitor, and so forth.

Let's call the first of these choices "active inaction." As noted earlier, while the self-destruct alarm continues to go crazy, the player can run his or her character all over Andrew Ryan's office and do anything that can be done in what we might call the "normal game state": jump, shoot, change various in-game settings like what skills are active, and so on. Active inaction in the game would be like Plato's escaped prisoner running around in the outside world looking at things. For the escaped prisoner, after having borne the terrible trial of the ascent—the pain of his feet on the stones, the pain of his eyes at the unfamiliar bright light of the sun—this kind of active inaction would have its own great pleasures. In fact, the escaped prisoner may be tempted to stay outside and contemplate the sun, which Plato tells us represents the form of the Good.

For the player of *BioShock*, having spent the game to this point gaining abilities, the analogy might be firing off those abilities to her heart's content.

It is the *uselessness*, though, of active inaction that poses the problem both to the player of *BioShock* and to the Platonic escaped prisoner: to think about the sun and to fire lightning bolts at furniture are fine as far as they go, but are they really choices? The answer, of course, depends on the definition of "choice," for certainly those things are something that the player may select, and do, in preference to disarming the self-destruct sequence. But *BioShock* and Plato's cave demonstrate that even though active inaction may meet the obvious definition of "choice," the idea behind that definition, which the definition itself cannot capture, is not fulfilled by such things as thinking about the sun (the form of the Good) and making evanescent dents with virtual bullets.

The idea behind choice is what Andrew Ryan means when he says, "A man chooses." As erroneous as the normative tone of the sentiment is (who is he to say that a man is someone who chooses whereas someone who obeys is a slave?), it corresponds to our most deeply and instinctually held beliefs about who we are. Choosing doesn't mean doing nothing: choosing means doing something. To do nothing, active inaction, fails to advance the world, just as it fails to advance the game state.

Meaningful choice is choice that has something to do with the possibility space. That's why the philosophers of *Republic* have to come back down to the cave—the cave is culture, the place where significant ethical action takes place.

What About Refusal?

The second way to avoid disarming the self-destruct sequence is to stop playing the game. I call this "refusal." Even better than the choice of active inaction, the choice of refusal exposes the basic flaw that both the cave and *BioShock* point out in the very concept of choice, both as we conceive it in our own lives and as it exists in particular cultural fields like video games and philosophy. To refuse to play the game negates the possibility space of *BioShock* as a stage for ethical critique, the same way as ceasing to read Plato negates the reader's capacity to engage in the critique of culture that Plato makes the purpose of the practice of the love of wisdom (that is, philosophy itself).

Refusal is a choice that negates choice even more thoroughly than the game and the cave do. We could take upon us what the great Greek tragedian Aeschylus (525–456 BCE) calls the "yoke of necessity" to disarm the self-destruct sequence, because we must do so to continue in the possibility and make future choices that feel more like choices. But if we instead refuse *BioShock* itself, and put down the controller, we have acknowledged that the state of manhood, as defined by Andrew Ryan's "a man chooses," does not include players of *BioShock*, because players of *BioShock* cannot make meaningful choices.

Thus, the non-choice of disarming the self-destruct sequence ends up in the same place as the other, more famous ethical dilemma of *BioShock*; that is, the choice of whether to harvest the Little Sisters or to save them. That's the part that everyone really, really gets wrong where *BioShock* is concerned, and so it's the part where comparing the game to Plato's cave can really help us get both of them right.

Harvest vs. Rescue: Stroke of Genius, Not a Flaw

Famously, to make the "evil" choice and harvest the Little Sisters and to make the "good" choice to save them end up functionally equivalent within the game mechanics, because the loss of ADAM attendant on saving them is made up by gifts from Dr. Tenenbaum. Generally, critics have viewed this equivalence between the choices as a flaw in the game's ethical system. In fact, just as Plato's cave culture, with its contests among the prisoners, shows how the choices presented to us by our experiences in culture are meaningless, so too does the game-mechanical equivalence of harvest and save. Seemingly ethical choices in games are meaningless, because those choices exist within a possibility space whose very nature is to constrain the player's choices within the predetermined limits of the game's rule set.

But it's where we can go from there that makes the project of bringing the cave and *BioShock* together worthwhile. The thing that happens inside the cave—the shadow-puppet play that makes up the entirety of the cultural world of the prisoners—is specifically designed by Plato to help us figure out things like video games. The culture of the cave is a shadow-puppet play for the very good reason that a shadow-puppet play is a form of playing pretend, what Plato calls *mimesis*. Mimesis in *Republic* is a very complicated subject, but playing pretend is the best way to think about it in both the positive and the negative lights in which Plato is trying to cast it: negative because Plato thinks that when you pretend to be bad you become bad; positive because doing it right (pretending to be good, for example) can help you learn more effectively than just about anything else.

Playing pretend is what they do in the cave; it's also what we do when we play *BioShock*. If we didn't have the cave to which to compare *BioShock*, we might well despair not just of the possibility of meaningful choice existing, but also of the possibility of doing anything meaningful about it. That's where *Republic* itself, and the rest of Plato's dialogues, come in. It's the reason Plato wrote in dialogue form in the first place.

One of the other things about *Republic* that people generally ignore is the way the entire thing is framed. Socrates tells the story of a conversation he had in an old guy's house. When you remember that ancient readers regarded reading silently either as impossible or at least as a very odd thing to do, you realize that the reader of *Republic* has to play pretend as Socrates, who is himself playing pretend both as himself and as the people he had his conversation with. That is, doing Platonic philosophy itself involves playing pretend, doing mimesis, but of a different kind from the kind engaged in by the prisoners of the cave.

Pretending to Talk about It

We can't avoid playing pretend. We can't avoid games. For one thing, they're fun. But if we want to have something to do about our possibility spaces, we need to play pretend with more purpose, and we need to pretend to talk about it. That's not a joke. We can definitely actually talk about it, of course, but what Plato saw is that it's even more important to *pretend* to talk about it, to stage ourselves as people who talk about this stuff. To play philosophers.

How does that work when you're playing *BioShock*? Actually, it's a lot easier when you're playing a video game than it is when you're reading a Platonic dialogue. Do stuff. Talk about stuff. Listen to the audio diaries in different orders, or while you're fighting a boss, or while you're fighting a Big Daddy. Equip a set of tonics that makes an ironic comment on the importance of the shooting mechanic to the *BioShock* games.

Everything you do as a player of a video game talks about that video game, if you're willing to see actions as having significance in the same way words do. If you were to capture what you were doing on a video, you could spell it out for an audience, the same way Plato has Socrates, at his most memorable moments, take apart the dialogue in which he's been engaged, dissecting the rhetorical strategies his interlocutors have been using.

But it all begins with the dialogue, with the playing pretend in the cave, just as doing philosophy in *BioShock*, when we see the possibility space of the game as a cave like Plato's cave, begins with playing the game. Pretending to do philosophy, in Plato or in *BioShock*, may in the end be the only thing that can lead us toward actually doing philosophy.

BioShock Infinite and Transworld Individuality
Identity across Space and Time

Charles Joshua Horn

Elizabeth: See? Not stars. They're doors.
Booker: Doors to…?
Elizabeth: To everywhere.

In the massive plot twist at the end of *BioShock Infinite*, the writers beautifully put forth a hypothesis that individuals might exist in more than one possible world. In philosophy, the idea that an individual can exist in more than one world is called transworld identity. An important rival to transworld identity theory is counterpart theory, the idea that individuals cannot exist in more than one possible world and are therefore "world bound."

But before we begin our discussion of individuals in different possible worlds, we need to be clear about just how *BioShock* treats possible worlds and how philosophers treat possible worlds. In *BioShock Infinite*, possible worlds are accessed through different lighthouses. These lighthouses represent ways in which the universe could be different than it is. The "infinite" in *BioShock Infinite* refers to the plurality of ways that the universe (what philosophers refer to as "worlds") could be. This modal theme permeates the game through the choices that the protagonist, Booker DeWitt, makes. In short, the idea expressed is that for every choice that someone makes, a new world is created wherein an alternative choice is made.

For philosophers who endorse a framework of possible worlds, there are two fundamentally different ways to think about them.[1] The

BioShock and Philosophy: Irrational Game, Rational Book, First Edition. Edited by Luke Cuddy.
© 2015 John Wiley & Sons, Inc. Published 2015 by John Wiley & Sons, Inc.

majority of philosophers who accept possible worlds are called actualists. According to these thinkers, there is an infinite set of ways that the world could be and only one of them (the world we live in) *really* exists in the most robust sense. Although it is contentious what makes the actual world actual, actualists generally agree that the other possible worlds are abstract.[2] Possible worlds, one of which is the actual world, might be represented as states of affairs, sets of propositions, collections of possible essences, and so on. One way in which we could think of the actualist position is that there were an infinite number of possible worlds that could have come into existence, and for whatever reason, only one possibility was made actual.

The second major division among philosophers who accept a framework of possible worlds is represented by possibilists. The most popular theory of possibilism is called modal realism. Modal realism is the thesis according to which there is an infinite number of possible worlds that *really* exist in the most robust sense, relative to themselves. So whereas the actualist is only willing to concede that there is one actual world, the possibilist will grant that the actual world could vary depending on the perspective of the world.

The world of Columbia is one possible world. The world of Rapture is another possible world. Both the actualist and the possibilist agree on these claims. However, the possibilist makes an additional claim, which is that from the perspective of Columbia or Rapture, those worlds are the actual world and our world is merely a possible world.

Why Should We Care?

Robert: Why do you ask what?
Rosalind: When the delicious question is when.
Robert: The only difference between past and present...
Rosalind: is semantics.
Robert: Lives, lived, will live.
Rosalind: Dies, died, will die.
Robert: If we could perceive time as it really was...
Rosalind: what reason would grammar professors have to get out of bed?
Robert: Like us all, Lady Comstock exists across time.
Rosalind: She is both alive and dead.
Robert: She perceives being both.
Rosalind: She finds this condition... disagreeable.

Although *BioShock Infinite* does a magnificent job at highlighting the plurality of worlds that might exist, it is unclear whether there is a coherent theory of transworld identity. That is, it is unclear whether or not one individual can be identical to another individual in a different world. But why should we care about transworld individuality at all? Traditionally, philosophers have cared about these issues because they help to explain other issues in metaphysics. Most important to the themes present in *BioShock*, transworld individuality has profound implications for differing notions of freedom. Other chapters in this volume sort out the issues of freedom in the *BioShock* universe, but it is important for the purposes of this chapter to show how vital a discussion of transworld individuality is for other areas of philosophy.

Using the framework of possible worlds, we can say that x is free to do y if and only if there is a possible world where x does y. For example, Booker was free to go to Columbia if there is at least one possible world where Booker goes to Columbia.[3] Implicit in this example, though, is the question of whether the Booker who goes to Columbia is identical to the Booker who does not go to Columbia.

In the seventeenth and eighteenth centuries, the question of transworld individuality was absolutely crucial, not only for issues of freedom, but, even more importantly, for moral responsibility. The theologian and philosopher Antoine Arnauld (1612–94) held that individuals must be identical in different possible worlds or else we could not be punished or rewarded for our free actions. Arnauld would claim, for example, that Booker's actions at Wounded Knee were free because there is also a possible world where Booker does not commit those atrocities. Most importantly, those two Bookers are identical to each other even though they exist in different possible worlds. Further, since the action was free, Booker can be held responsible for those actions.

It would be very unfair, Arnauld would argue, to be held morally responsible for an action if one could not have done otherwise. Suppose that there is no possible world in which Booker exists where he does not commit the atrocities at Wounded Knee. That is, assume that it is necessary that Booker committed the atrocities at Wounded Knee. We would be hard pressed, Arnauld would think, to be able to explain how we can justify punishing Booker for something that he *had* to do.

The philosopher Gottfried Leibniz (1646–1716) had a famous correspondence with Arnauld about this very issue. Whereas Arnauld had endorsed transworld individuality, Leibniz could not. We can hold Booker responsible for his actions at Wounded Knee not because there is another possible world wherein he does not do those actions (strictly speaking, this is false for Leibniz), but because Booker's decision was self-motivated; that is, it came from his own will.

Essentialism

Elizabeth: We swim in different oceans but land on the same shore.

The fundamental disagreement between Arnauld and Leibniz has to do with their respective views of essentialism. Although the thesis is nuanced (as we will see shortly), it is generally agreed that essentialism is the view according to which at least some of the properties that make up an individual are essential to him or her. The question, then, in this discussion is: "What properties are essential or necessary to an individual?" There are three basic answers to this question.

First, we could hold that no properties are essential to an individual. This position, sometimes referred to as anti-essentialism, means that there isn't one property of Booker, for instance, that identifies him in different possible worlds. Booker could be Comstock, Elizabeth, Songbird, or even a lighthouse. Booker cannot be identified with the fact that he is male, organic, or even human. In short, Booker could lose *all* of his properties and still be Booker.

Second, we could hold that all properties are essential to an individual. This position, sometimes referred to as "superessentialism," means that every property of Booker is necessary for his existence. If Booker were to lack even one property that defines his being, then it would not be Booker. So if Booker were a woman, then it would not be Booker. If Booker were not human, then it would not be Booker. Further, since our choices define who we are, every choice is necessary to Booker's essence. If Booker did not go to Columbia, then it would not be Booker. If Booker did not commit the atrocities at Wounded Knee, then it would not be Booker.

Third, we could maintain an intermediate position, namely that some of the properties of an individual are essential to him or her. This position, sometimes referred to as moderate essentialism, entails that some properties are essential and some are not. Unfortunately, there is wide disagreement among philosophers about which kind of properties are essential. We might say, for example, that Booker's hairstyle is not essential to his being, but his choices are. Or, we might say that Booker's occupation is not essential to his being, but his beliefs are. The burden of moderate essentialists, though, is to explain why some properties are more important than others.

As we saw earlier, it is highly contested among philosophers (even those who are willing to accept the possible worlds lingo) whether individuals can exist in more than one world. Given our analysis of essentialism, we can start to piece together how certain views would entail other positions about modality. Since the anti-essentialist maintains that there are no properties of an individual that are necessary to him or her, it is easy to understand how individuals can exist differently in other possible worlds. Booker can be completely different in another world and still be Booker. Similarly, since a moderate essentialist maintains that some properties are not essential to the individual, the very same individual can exist in other possible worlds. However, a superessentialist believes that individuals are world-bound; that is, they only exist in their own world—not other possible worlds. This must follow because if every property is essential to the individual, then there would be no way to individuate one individual in one world from another individual in another world.[4]

Transworld Identity and Counterpart Theory

Rosalind Lutece: When I was a girl, I dreamt of standing in a room, looking at a girl who was and was not myself, who stood looking at another girl who was and was not myself. My mother took this as a nightmare. I saw it as the beginning of a career in physics.

With a basic groundwork of possible worlds in place, we are now in a position to evaluate the *BioShock* games in terms of whether a coherent theory of transworld identity or counterpart theory is present. By way of reminder, transworld identity stipulates that an individual x can exist in world W_1 and an individual y can exist in world W_2 and that x is identical to y. By contrast, counterpart theory stipulates that x and y are not identical in this case, but can be counterparts of one another depending on the strictness of our similarity relation.

The earlier discussion regarding actualism and possibilism is important, because if we are going to talk about individuals existing in worlds, then we need to be clear about what kinds of things worlds are. Transworld identity is a much easier thesis to accept for a possibilist because modal realism holds that other possible worlds are concrete in just the way that the actual world is concrete. Things are much more complicated for an actualist with regard to transworld identity. After all, it is initially unclear how an individual in the actual world could be identical to an abstract entity. To address this problem, many actualists re-conceive what it means to exist in a possible world. Rather than think of other possible worlds as concrete entities, actualists tend to think of a possible world as a world that might have been actual, but was not.

Even though transworld identity is easier to accept for a possibilist, the standard account of modal realism denies that individuals can be identical across possible worlds. Instead, it endorses a version of counterpart theory. The reason for this is the logical law of identity. It is illogical to suppose that an individual in one world can have a certain set of properties that is different from the individual to whom they are identical in another possible world. For example, if we suppose that Booker in one world is identical with Comstock in another, and also that Booker and Comstock have different properties, then they cannot be identical. After all, if two things are identical, then they share all of their properties (according to the principle of the indiscernibility of identicals).

To address this problem, modal realists tend to accept a counterpart theory that is based on similarity, but not identity. In this sense, an individual can be a counterpart of another individual in a different possible world if the individuals are sufficiently similar in the appropriate way. So the question remains, what kind of modal theories does *BioShock Infinite* seem to accept?

Insofar as Columbia, Rapture, and an infinite number of other possible worlds are depicted as concrete places and not abstract entities, this seems to be evidence for a version of modal realism. Nevertheless, there are a few objections to what might otherwise seem like an obvious answer. Perhaps most significantly, modal realists tend to identify possible worlds as isolated in space and time. This means that it is metaphysically impossible to get to another possible world.[5] Since one of the major story and gameplay mechanics in *BioShock Infinite* is that the player can manipulate tears in space and time through Elizabeth, we should be careful about attributing possibilism to the series. Nevertheless, possibilism is a much better fit for *BioShock Infinite* than actualism, and, as such, a counterpart theoretic model seems most fitting.

Counterparts in the World of *BioShock*

> Elizabeth: They're a million million worlds. All different and all similar. Constants and variables.

To demonstrate the counterpart theory, consider three pivotal figures in the *BioShock* universe: Booker DeWitt, Elizabeth Comstock, and the Lutece twins.

First, in one of the final revelations of the game, the player finds out that Booker DeWitt is a counterpart of Zachary Comstock, the Prophet and founder of Columbia. Comstock is the manifestation of Booker when he was baptized after the battle of Wounded Knee. The two characters are clear counterparts because they share a plurality of properties and are differentiated in the story merely by the choice to be baptized. The origins of their life up to the baptism are identical, their bodies are mostly identical, their relations to others are identical, and so forth.

Second, when Booker is tasked with delivering the young Anna DeWitt to Comstock to expunge his gambling debts, he changes his mind at the last moment and tries to keep her in his own world. In one of the most significant moments of the game, Anna's finger becomes severed, part of it stays in Booker's world, and the rest goes along with Anna into Comstock's reality. As a result, Anna DeWitt exists in multiple realities. Again, we have a clear case of a counterpart. Like Booker and Comstock, Anna and Elizabeth share similar origins, bodies, relation to others, and so forth. Elizabeth Comstock, Anna DeWitt's counterpart, is not the only character in *BioShock Infinite* to exist in different possible worlds, though.

Finally, and perhaps most obvious to the discussion of counterparts, we have the ubiquitous and mysterious Lutece twins. In the game, Rosalind was a quantum physicist with primary areas of research in other possible worlds. During her research, she was able to communicate with her "twin" in another possible reality—a counterpart named Robert. When the Luteces tried to help Elizabeth so that the prophecy foretelling the destruction of New York City would not occur, Comstock ordered Jeremiah Fink to sabotage the machine that the Luteces were using to create the tears in reality. Instead of the twins being killed, though, they gained the ability to exist in all possible worlds. This is an even clearer case of counterparts, because the existence of Robert Lutece comes directly from Rosalind.

In one of the most significant revelations in the game, Elizabeth leads Booker to a place that exists outside of space and time (at least in the traditional sense) and contains an infinite set of lighthouses—doors to other realities. One of these realities was the world from the previous *BioShock* entries, Rapture. Compellingly, philosophical issues of identity do not manifest from one game alone, but across different games. Not only does Booker have a counterpart in Comstock, he also has a counterpart in Jack, the protagonist from the first game. In what might be very easily overlooked, the original *BioShock* indicates that only Andrew Ryan can operate the bathyspheres. Because Jack is connected to Andrew Ryan, he can operate them too. But what happens when Elizabeth takes Booker to Rapture to escape Songbird? He operates the bathysphere just like Jack! The analogy works on a different level, too. Since Booker is a counterpart of Jack, it could also be the case that Comstock is a counterpart of Andrew Ryan, since both of them can technically operate the bathyspheres. Further, since the counterpart relation is based on a similarity relation that could change, it might be argued that there are other trans-game counterparts such as the Big Daddy and Songbird, Dr. Tenenbaum and Dr. Lutece, and also Fontaine and Daisy Fitzroy.

BioShock and Necessary Beings

Elizabeth: There's always a lighthouse, there's always a man, there's always a city…

Part of what makes *BioShock* great is that so much of each story is left to thoughtful players to piece together themselves. Much of what I have presented here is not explicit in the games, but nevertheless seems to follow from what we do know about their universe. *BioShock Infinite* is particularly exciting to both philosophy and the series because it brilliantly depicts a way in which prior games fit into the larger picture, while also laying a foundation for possible future stories to come. It should not be lost on the player and reader that there are seemingly an infinite number of stories, which manifest in different ways. Having said that, if we take Elizabeth at her word that there is *always* a lighthouse, a man, and a city, then *BioShock* is depicting something that philosophers have been grappling with for thousands of years; namely, the existence of God.

Philosophers traditionally conceive of God as a necessary being. Given our framework of possible worlds, this means that if God exists (as a necessary being), then he exists in all possible worlds. Put differently, if God exists, it is precisely his necessity that governs his existence in all possible worlds instead of only some possible worlds. But this is exactly the story that *BioShock* depicts; namely, the existence of necessary beings. The man, whether it is Jack or Booker, is a different manifestation of the same being. They are counterparts of one another. We might object here that the analogy isn't perfect, because Jack or Booker does not exist in all possible worlds and so can't fit the model of a necessary being. But then, what about the Lutece twins? The result of "dying" in their machine was that they were able to manifest in *any* reality whatsoever, not just Columbia. For all we know, it seems to be consistent with the reality of *BioShock* that they could appear in future representations of the city—not just Rapture or Columbia. In effect, they are necessary beings and satisfy at least one major component of the traditional conception of God.

The Plurality of Worlds to Come

Elizabeth: They're doors to everywhere. All that's left is the choosing.

In the metaphysics of modality, things become much more complicated than even the complex *BioShock* series depicts.[6] In the games, possible worlds exist based only on the choices that individuals make within those worlds. The logical possibilities are more vast than can manifest through choices alone. After all, it is possible that there is a world with nobody making choices at all! We might also wonder about the veridicality of Elizabeth's claim that there is always a lighthouse, a man, and a city. Is there really supposed to be a connection here to divinity? Or are the only worlds that we care about the ones that tell this basic story in different ways? Finally, even if we grant that there is a possible world for each new choice that people make in those worlds, why should we conclude that all possible Comstocks are destroyed once Booker allows Elizabeth to drown him at the end? By *BioShock*'s own logic, there should be a possible world where he does not allow Elizabeth to drown him, too.

Its far-reaching implications make *BioShock* such a worthy philosophical endeavor. The games connect issues in metaphysics, epistemology, ethics, aesthetics, and political theory to one strong story that manifests in a plurality of ways. Perhaps what is most exciting about *BioShock* is that even though an infinite number of possible stories are on the horizon, the series also asks the player to consider what we even mean when talking about what it means to be possible in the first place. In this way, *BioShock* at its best is akin to philosophy at its best. Both draw attention to certain presuppositions that we take for granted. Not everything is possible. But *BioShock* certainly makes us reconsider traditional answers associated with the question.[7]

Notes

1. For more on this, see Peter van Inwagen, "Two Concepts of Possible Worlds," *Midwest Studies in Philosophy* 11 (1986): 185–213.
2. For more on this, see Robert Adams, "Theories of Actuality," *Noûs* 8 (1974): 211–231.
3. At least, according to a standard libertarian account of free will.
4. Of course, this also requires us to accept certain other Leibnizian principles, such as the Principle of Sufficient Reason and the Identity of Indiscernibles. For the purposes of simplicity and brevity, I've left these out of the main discussion.
5. Philosophers distinguish metaphysical impossibility from other kinds of impossibility such as physical, technological, alethic, or nomological impossibility. Metaphysical impossibility is sometimes thought about in terms of when propositions are consistent, that is, not containing contradictions. It would be metaphysically impossible, for instance, for Songbird to kill Booker *and* for Songbird *not* to kill Booker. One, and only one, proposition must be true.
6. For a more detailed discussion of possible worlds, see my "Dreams and Possible Worlds: *Inception* and the Metaphysics of Modality," in *Inception and Philosophy: Because It's Never Just a Dream*, ed. David Kyle Johnson (Hoboken, NJ: John Wiley & Sons, 2011), 215–230.
7. I would like to thank Luke Cuddy and Bill Irwin for their helpful comments on earlier versions of this chapter. This is written for my gamer friends and loved ones who introduced me to the world of *BioShock*. Here's hoping that for any possible world in which I exist, Tyler Horn, Ed Sorrell, Shane Beasley, and Jonathan and Joshua Keeton exist too.

9

Shockingly Limited
Escaping Columbia's God of Necessity

Scott Squires and James McBain

At the end of *BioShock Infinite,* Booker is faced with the challenge of not allowing the tragedy to befall Columbia. There has to be a way, he believes, to prevent the rise of Father Comstock, the imprisonment and abuse of Elizabeth, and the creation of a Columbia that persecutes people for both religious and racial reasons. Booker tells Elizabeth, who is at the height of her powers of seeing through time and space, that he will do anything to prevent Comstock from coming to power. Elizabeth takes him back to Father Comstock's creation and it is revealed that Comstock's coming to power took place when DeWitt accepted Christian baptism after his participation in the Wounded Knee massacre. Booker is Comstock! The shock of this revelation hits the player as the narrative plays out. Booker is given the opportunity to destroy Comstock, as Elizabeth, his own daughter, takes him back to that moment—drowning himself in the waters of baptism as all the Elizabeths from all the possible worlds watch. Booker dies. Elizabeth, Comstock, and Columbia disappear. *Fin.*

We are left with a lingering metaphysical question, though. Did Booker *have* to become Comstock? The question is more difficult than it seems. In all the possible worlds that are shown, the creation of Columbia and the birth and imprisonment of Anna/Elizabeth are consequences of this particular action. On Booker's acceptance of drowning in the baptismal waters, Columbia and Elizabeth fade away,

BioShock and Philosophy: Irrational Game, Rational Book, First Edition. Edited by Luke Cuddy.
© 2015 John Wiley & Sons, Inc. Published 2015 by John Wiley & Sons, Inc.

as do the consequences of them existing. Booker's action is predicated on the necessity of Booker becoming Comstock.

The notion that Booker DeWitt had to become Father Comstock because of his baptism (and that only death could prevent this transformation) portrays a God that is overly deterministic, however. In reality, God may be omnipotent and omniscient, and yet humans may be free. Just because God knows what choices human beings will make with their free will does not necessarily mean that we are not free.[1] In the end, Booker DeWitt never *had* to become Father Comstock, just as those who are devoted to God never have to become dangerous extremists.

Determinism, Necessity, and the "Infinite" in *BioShock Infinite*

While moving through the game, the player encounters tears, rips in the fabric of space–time. Both Booker and Elizabeth can see the tears, but only Elizabeth can interact and move through them. On the other side of the tears are alternative universes. A better way to put this is that the tears represent possible worlds, representations of possible situations. Generally, possible worlds are expressed as sets of consistent descriptions. Any world is possible as long as it is internally coherent and does not contain (or entail) any contradictions. There is a possible world for any possible description of some state of affairs. There is a possible world in which the authors did not write this chapter, but juggled chainsaws instead. There is a possible world in which you're fiercely battling a Big Daddy instead of reading this chapter. There are as many possible worlds as there are consistent sets of descriptions. Indeed, there is an infinite number of possible worlds. So, we can think of each tear around Columbia as showing the way to one of those possible worlds. Are possible worlds real worlds? Do they exist? Although philosophers debate this issue, we can set it aside here. For in Columbia, possible worlds are real, concrete worlds.

That Booker has to become Comstock suggests that there are only two possibilities—Booker becomes Comstock or Booker dies. This disjunction has to be true; it is *necessarily* true. Necessity is often cashed out in terms of possible worlds. If there is no possible world in which some sentence or proposition doesn't hold, then we can say that sentence or proposition is necessarily true. If there is no possible world in which the sentence or proposition holds, the sentence is necessarily false. If there are some possible worlds in which it's true and some in which it's false, then it is contingently true. In *BioShock Infinite*, there are no possible worlds in which either Booker becomes Comstock and dies, or Booker doesn't become Comstock and doesn't die.

If it is necessarily the case that either Booker becomes Comstock or he dies, then some people will say that he couldn't do otherwise. It looks like the universe of *BioShock Infinite* is deterministic. The American philosopher William James (1842–1910) described determinism in this way: "those parts of the universe already laid down absolutely appoint and decree what the other parts shall be... [t]he future has no ambiguous possibilities hidden in its womb."[2]

Limiting Possibilities Means There Is No Real *Infinite*

In *BioShock Infinite* there is no world where Columbia, Father Comstock, the Vox Populi, and Elizabeth do not exist. There is no Columbia that exists with any other kind of religious or social direction. By the end of the game, if Booker wants to prevent harm and suffering to others, he is left with one option: die in the waters of baptism. The baptism that Booker accepted was a distinctly Christian one. Traditionally, this would mean that Booker was to have an opportunity for a new life, a clean slate to write on. Instead, the only outcome we see is Booker becoming Comstock. Elizabeth fading away when Booker dies further enforces this idea. The game is indicating that Comstock is a necessary outcome of Booker accepting baptism; this is determined to be the case unless he dies at a critical point in his life or doesn't exist at all. There is also no way for Elizabeth to exist in any of these worlds, as she (and her male counterparts in other worlds) will fade away when you die. Furthermore, there is the possible interpretation that in the *BioShock* world, public acts of religious devotion necessarily lead to religious extremism.

Attempting to Reconcile the Infinite

In *BioShock Infinite*, God is all-powerful (omnipotent) and all-knowing (omniscient). God would also be timeless or eternal according to the traditional Christian conception.[3] In relation to this God, we are at an extreme disadvantage. We are in time, limited in our ability to know, and not as powerful as we think we are. So, if there is going to be any interaction between God and the people of Columbia (or the rest of us), then it will have to come from God's abilities and not our own.

In order to interact with humans, God has to enter into the reality of the *BioShock* universe, or into our reality somehow. But God has already entered into our reality. For the universe to be in a traditionally Christian sense, God invested God's own self into it at creation. In doing this, God, while distinct from the creation, became so close to it that it is as though the creation were suspended in God. God is omnipresent not just because God encompasses creation, but because God is all throughout it as well. While some people may think this is pantheism (which means that God *is* everything), it is actually pan*en*theism (which means that God is *in* everything), because while God is everywhere throughout creation, God is still distinct from creation.

The thought that God could be everywhere throughout our world can then lead to some interesting possibilities when it comes to the outcome of the universe. It could be that because God is throughout every place and every time, there is nothing that is going to happen that God is not making happen. This would lead to the determinism that is presented with the life of Booker DeWitt. But it could also mean that God allows for us to help determine the outcome of things. God could still be omniscient, knowing the possible outcomes of all things, but not causing or determining them.

There are two reasons that this makes sense. The first is that in order for there to be justice, there must be free will. There must be the possibility that we could have chosen differently. Otherwise, there would be no justice in the punishment or reward for choices made. In the Christian sense, God would not be just in punishing people eternally or rewarding them eternally if the choices that we made in this life were not free. The second reason is the emphasis (especially in Christianity, but also seen throughout most forms of divine/human interaction in other religions) concerning prayer. If God has the universe pre-decided, then why should people ask about changing the outcome of anything? Christians are told to pray for many things, including protection and healing. An Old Testament story (2 Kings 20:1–11) sees a king told by God that he is going to die from the sickness he has and then, after he prays, God says that he does not have to die, but can live another 20 years. An intricate part of the God/man interaction hinges on prayer, thus showing that the universe is not fully determined.

God, as defined here, is still omniscient. God can still see all ends from all beginnings and still know what course the universe will take. But the universe can still be indeterminate, because God doesn't violate the autonomy inherent in our choices by determining what they shall be. People could both reject or accept the saving grace of God (as DeWitt does in the game) and still take actions that are not predetermined, because God is letting humans have the choice.

With this understanding of God, we have a very different possible outcome for *BioShock Infinite*. Booker DeWitt could have accepted baptism and made different choices that would have allowed him to be a good father to Elizabeth while remaining devoted to God. Becoming a "new creature" by going into the waters of baptism did not take away any of the choices that DeWitt had in his future. At any point, Booker could have opted out of becoming Father Comstock. If Booker has real choice, then the "Infinite" in the title of the game is accurate. Perhaps there is a world where Booker is happily married and raising Elizabeth to follow the Christian faith to which he became devoted after Wounded Knee. Perhaps there is a Columbia where DeWitt is not using Elizabeth for his own ends, but rather letting her decide how to help keep this floating city in the sky, a sort of "father–daughter" partnership as opposed to the imprisonment model. Or maybe there is a Columbia that is ethnically diverse the way the Church is called to be by St. Paul in the letter to the Ephesians. As the game is now, the idea of infinite possible worlds may apply, but the idea of truly infinite possibilities is not present, because of the necessity and determinism that the Booker DeWitt/Father Comstock character displays. As currently constructed, the game leads to a shockingly limited outcome. Really, if openness is factored into God's dealings with humanity, DeWitt could have lived a deeply devoted religious life without becoming the dangerous zealot Father Comstock, because God is allowing man the choice not to step over that line between deeply devoted and dangerous zealot.

Religious Extremism and the *BioShock Infinite* Narrative

The ending of *BioShock Infinite* is potentially problematic for another reason. The narrative can be read as reinforcing the idea that if one is devoted to God, then one will be led to dangerous religious extremism. Comstock is presented as a visionary, a motivating and charismatic public speaker on a divine mission. He obviously has the ability to organize and delegate to see his vision realized, as we can see in the creation of glorious Columbia. Comstock has many admirable qualities that we would prize in the actual world, but, unchecked, these qualities lead to horrible outcomes. Comstock is a racist, willing to go to any lengths to see his vision become a reality, even if that means imprisoning his daughter or taking someone's life because of his or her ethnic heritage.

Comstock is portrayed in a manner that suggests, if he is to exist at all, then he necessarily must have these awful traits. The problem with this portrayal, though, is that it reinforces the idea that if people are going to be devoted to God, then they will be dangerous and extreme. This is a distorted view of what it means to be religious, regardless of the religion.

Adult Christian baptism is a very public ritual and, if done with understanding, is an event that will forever mark a Christian's life. The one who is getting baptized is making a public commitment to leave behind an old way of life for a new one. The *BioShock* game designers did a very good job getting that part right. There is definitely a sense when a player first enters Columbia through baptism and later at the scene of Booker's baptism that one has to leave the old life behind. This is the essence of Christian baptism, living a different life. But one can live a different life without being racist or elitist like Comstock (and really most of the other denizens of Columbia). Accepting Christian baptism means that one is going to try to model the Christian God's character on a daily basis. And it is hard to see the character of such a God looking like Comstock.

This distortion of what it means to be publicly devoted to the Christian God might be fueled by fears that have their roots in the actions of those who claim to be doing God's will by hurting or killing others in the name of God. The 9/11 attacks on the USA are an example of this kind of "Comstock devotion." The hijackers thought that they were doing Allah's will by taking away the autonomy of those on the planes and killing thousands of people, thereby showing the depth of their devotion. Bombing and killing others is not the way that most Muslims live, however, and to say that all of them must act in this way or they are not true Muslims would be an insult to all peace-loving Muslims. Christian extremists who bomb abortion clinics and protest at the funerals of dead American soldiers likewise exhibit a "Comstock devotion." With the media attention that is a constant part of our culture, these are the people who make the news and they are the ones who end up defining in the minds of many what it means to be "devoted to God." These examples of religious extremism may be part of why Comstock is portrayed this way.

Deep devotion to God is radical in nature and can lead to extreme results, but that does not mean that these results have to be dangerous. Through the centuries many people have lost their lives due to their public commitment to God. For example, Anabaptists were killed by both the Catholics and the Protestants of the 1500s for their commitment to the idea that baptism had to be something that one chose to do with understanding. Many of the Jewish faith have been killed because of their commitment and refusal to bow before anything else than the one God. This kind of devotion obviously does not mean that one has to take someone else's life or violate their autonomy in order to be devoted. The *BioShock Infinite* ending says that Booker had to become a person who would do these very things and that this was determined to be the case in every world in which he existed. However, it didn't have to be that way if Booker DeWitt had a real choice.

In the end, one really can live a life of deep religious devotion to God without becoming a dangerous religious extremist who must hurt people to prove that devotion. The picture we get of one who is deeply religiously devoted to the point that he would accept baptism as a sign of that devotion is one that leaves a bad taste in our mouths when it comes to religion. This picture reinforces the idea that religion will lead to awful events like the Crusades of the Middle Ages or the jihads of recent years. It reinforces the idea that religion is for the unreasonable, and that any kind of devotion to God will lead to dangerous outcomes that no reasonable person would endorse.

Final Thoughts

The final scenes of Booker DeWitt having to drown himself to prevent this monster Comstock from rising are sad, not because he has to kill himself and his daughter to be a hero and prevent all kinds of bad things from happening, but because he didn't have to. Choice is a real thing and Comstock didn't have to come into being. Even if God really can see the end from the beginning and has the power to do all things, this does not compromise human freedom.

Notes

1. For this chapter we will be focusing on a Christian conception of God and in the game Comstock makes reference to the "lamb of God" and other Christian ideas. However, our analysis would apply to any monotheistic conception of God.
2. William James, "The Will to Believe," Project Gutenberg. http://www.gutenberg.org/files/26659/26659-h/26659-h.htm.
3. Again, we are focusing on the Christian conception of God given the game's narrative. However, any monotheistic account that accepts God being omnipotent and omniscient would apply.

Part III
THE "UNION" AND THE SODOM BELOW

10

"The bindings are there as a safeguard"
Sovereignty and Political Decisions in *BioShock Infinite*

Rick Elmore

BioShock Infinite begins with the question of "founding." One enters Columbia for the first time on "Secession Day," the anniversary of Columbia's secession from the United States in 1902, and the commemoration of the founding of Columbia as the "New Eden." In order to enter the city, however, players (as Booker DeWitt) must be baptized, a symbolic refounding of the individual as a new, "saved" person.

Founding is an age-old problem in political philosophy, the question of how one establishes a legitimate legal and political system. For much of human history, this legitimacy was thought to come from God, leaders claiming a right to rule as a representative of the divine. But ever since the Enlightenment and its emphasis on personal freedom, democracy, and the secular state, there has been a push to see political legitimacy as coming from other sources, like power, the people, law, or science. This change raised new problems for political theory, not the least of which is beautifully captured in one of the first Voxophone recordings that players encounter in *BioShock Infinite*.

In the Voxophone entitled "Every Man All at Once," Comstock says of baptism:

> one man goes into the waters of baptism. A different man comes out, born again. But who is that man who lies submerged? Perhaps that swimmer is both sinner and saint, until he is revealed unto the eyes of man.

BioShock and Philosophy: Irrational Game, Rational Book, First Edition. Edited by Luke Cuddy.
© 2015 John Wiley & Sons, Inc. Published 2015 by John Wiley & Sons, Inc.

In the moment before an individual emerges from the waters of baptism, she is both sinner and saint, neither clearly saved nor clearly damned. This ambiguity of baptism is the very ambiguity at the heart of secular political founding. The problem with founding a new legal order is that the moment of that founding is logically prior to the legal order itself, since you have to establish laws before you can practice them. However, this means that the founding of the law is always outside the law and is, therefore, not legal. Every founding of a new law is from the beginning unjustifiable within the legal order that it founds.

"No, But I'm Afraid of You" — Booker DeWitt

The result of this problematic logic is that it seems to throw a wrench into the possibility of founding a legitimate secular and democratic state. If no constitutional democracy can justify its constitutional legality, then from where does its legitimacy come? This is the question that Comstock's first Voxophone asks us to consider: From where does legitimacy come? In the non-secular state, the answer to this question was easy: God. However, with secular states we need a new answer. This issue is even more complicated for democratic states, since the power that founds them must itself be democratic, in order to avoid the embarrassing notion of a democracy based on an undemocratic exercise of power or military force. Hence, the desire to ground the legitimacy of the secular state is one of the defining problems of modern political and democratic theory, and it is also the question with which *BioShock Infinite* begins. OK. So what do we do with this conundrum?

One of the best-known and most influential attempts to solve the problem of founding was proposed by the German political theorist Carl Schmitt (1888–1985), who argued that all political communities are based on "the antithesis between friend and enemy."[1] For Schmitt, it isn't constitutional or legal arrangements that ground political communities, but divisions between antagonistic groups. The antagonisms between these groups can, Schmitt contends, come from any number of places: race, class, nationality, ideology, and so forth. However, the enemy has to be "in a specifically intense way, existentially something different and alien, so that in the extreme cases conflicts with him are

SOVEREIGNTY AND POLITICAL DECISIONS

possible."[2] The "enemy group" has to be different and alien enough to the "friend group" so that, in extreme circumstances, they would be willing to go to war with each other. On the basis of this fundamental antagonism, Schmitt argues that one can found legitimate secular states, since the fundamental antagonism between "the people" and their "enemy" constitutes a true and legitimate expression of the will of "the people." Hence, the legitimacy of the secular state rests, for Schmitt, on the power of the friend/enemy distinction to provide a basis for constitutional law. Yet a politics founded on an antagonism between friend and enemy groups is certainly not limited to democratic states, as is clear from the example of Columbia in *BioShock Infinite*.

Columbian society defines itself against a number of enemies in the Schmittian sense: the white supremacy, classism, secessionism, theocracy, and anti-democratic fervor of Columbia all mark defining antagonisms. Columbia's identity is solely based on its difference from the America below, which has, its people claim, become too accommodating to the non-white, lower-class, secular, and democratic. The first two-thirds of the game are a tour of these antagonisms from the racism of the Raffle and the Fraternal Order of the Raven, to the authoritarian patriotism of Duke and Dimwit, and the classism of Fink's docks and factory. Players see the racist underpinnings of Columbia's economic structure, and play through mock-ups of Wounded Knee and the Boxer Rebellion, events on which Columbia bases its claim to independence. Hence, *BioShock Infinite* exemplifies Schmitt's concept of the political, as grounded on fundamental antagonisms that express the will of "the people" (which is to say, the will of most of the well-to-do white people) of Columbia. However, Columbia's antagonisms also expose some of the tensions in Schmitt's understanding of politics.

The Vox

The game-defining political antagonism of *BioShock Infinite* is that between Comstock and the Vox Populi. Players learn of the Vox Populi and its leader, Daisy Fitzroy, early on from overheard conversations, Kinetoscopes, and, most explicitly, the carnival games on the way to the Raffle. The Vox is an underground resistance fighting against Comstock in the name of the oppressed people of Columbia. Their relationship with Comstock is a Schmittian antagonism in the truest sense, as they are more than willing to go to war with their political adversary. In the end, however, the Vox prove just as violently ideological and tyrannical as Comstock, a point hammered home when players must thwart Fitzroy's execution of Fink's young son, for nothing more than the "crime" of being his offspring. The antagonism between the Vox and Comstock leads, in the end, to a tyranny by the Vox.

Why this reversal? Is it the result of power-hungry leadership? Mistakes? Or the corrupting influence of power? Much in the game, particularly DeWitt's constant doubts about the Vox's true motives, points toward the last of these conclusions: the notion that political power always corrupts democratic and egalitarian ideals. This reversal raises doubts about the possibility of grounding democratic power on antagonism and conflict, as it seems to lead, at least in the case of the Vox, to anti-democratic results. However, this kind of reversal is logically entailed by a Schmittian notion of politics.

In Schmittian politics, the friend/enemy antagonism grounds political identity. It wholly defines the group identity of both friend and enemy. The result of this is that a positive political identity is impossible, since only opposition defines one's political identity: "we are what they aren't." This lack of a positive identity helps to explain the reversal of the Vox, since if one's identity is based purely on opposition to another group, the destruction of that group entails the destruction of one's own identity. What is the Vox Populi without Comstock? Without the tyranny of Comstock to define themselves against, the Vox lose all sense of themselves. They literally cannot survive without tyranny to fight against, so that when they overthrow the tyrant, they must immediately invent a new one (Fink's son), an invention that leads them ironically into tyranny themselves. So, from a Schmittian perspective, the Vox's reversal is not a mere accident of poor leadership or human nature, but is the logical consequence of conceiving politics in terms of a friend/enemy divide. Yet this dependence on an enemy is more than a merely theoretical problem, as illustrated in the racism of Columbia's economic system.

"Cherubs for Every Chore!" — Jeremiah Fink

Racial difference is one of the major antagonisms in *BioShock Infinite*. Columbia is a white supremacist society modeled on the segregationist past of the United States. The racist iconography of chattel slavery, the repression of Native Peoples, and hatred toward Asians and the Irish all invoke forms of racial violence historically found in the United States. In addition, the events that lead to Columbia's secession are the massacre at Wounded Knee (1890) and the Boxer Rebellion (1899–1901). Both of these events link political power and racial violence—Wounded Knee marking the end of large-scale resistance to the US government's theft and appropriation of Native lands; and the Boxer Rebellion marking a nationalist, anti-imperialist movement in China and the first time a US president sent troops overseas without congressional approval (in clear violation of the US Constitution, might I add). Hence, these events illustrate the collusion between racism, property rights, and constitutional authority. But, as players quickly discover, this racist antagonism is not merely political; it also grounds Columbia's entire economic structure.

Shortly after fighting through the first waves of police following the Raffle, players find a prominently placed Voxophone, which explains that Columbia's economy is run on a workforce of black penal labor from the state of Georgia. It turns out that while professing hatred, intolerance, and the exclusion of non-whites from Columbian society, Columbia is, in reality, entirely dependent on a mostly non-white labor force. In addition, racism and classism are aligned throughout, a connection made most explicit in the propaganda film on Fink's Dock, comparing owners to lions and workers to oxen, with the voiceover: "Oxen cannot become lions." One of the most powerful elements of this aspect of the game is its relation to the real history of the United States, whose economy was for many decades run on the labor of slaves and a system of slave plantations.

The questions of racism, classism, and wealth inequality remain pressing issues in American social and political life. However, in relationship to Schmitt's argument, one sees here that the logical dependency of the friend group on its enemy is also a material dependency, the friend group being unable to expel its enemy for want of their labor power. So racism proves to be much more than a mere political or social antagonism in *BioShock Infinite*, operating rather as the primary means of producing and maintaining economic stability. Now, certainly all the links here to US history challenge us to think about the connections between racism, classism, and economics in America. In addition, the material nature of the friend/enemy distinction should come as no surprise, given Schmitt's emphasis on the "existential" (meaning really existing) differences that this distinction entails.

However, this overall logic of dependence between the friend and the enemy creates a paradox in Schmitt's theory.

War without End

Schmitt's concept of the political leads to the paradoxical conclusion that the enemy group must be both expelled and included in political life. On this logic, politics becomes the strange operation of expelling the unexpellable or of continuously trying to expel the unexpellable. The result of this logic is that politics becomes a process of constant and endless war, constant because antagonism is the basis of all politics, and endless because one can't ever eliminate the need for an enemy group. In order to appreciate the importance and danger of this logic, one need go no further than the example of America's War on Terror, a war that seems endless, since there is no clearly defined enemy and, consequently, no way to identify victory. In the case of *BioShock Infinite*, it is in order to avoid precisely the ongoing and seemingly endless war with Comstock that players are driven finally to allow Anna to drown them (DeWitt), achieving victory by eliminating the very existence of Columbia, Comstock, and DeWitt. Here again, one can't help but wonder if this paradox doesn't spell disaster for the hope of grounding democratic and constitutional states, since a democracy run on a principle of war seems to foreclose "the people's" democratic ability to pursue peace. However, this question of the importance of choice in democratic life brings us to the other great legacy of Schmitt's political philosophy, and one of the most frequently discussed questions of modern political thought; namely, the concept of sovereignty.

Sovereignty is generally understood to be the power of an individual or organization over a geographic area. For example, all independent governments are thought to be sovereign, having the power to decide and execute all laws within their borders. Schmitt, however, defines the sovereign more specifically as "he who decides on the exception."[3] The sovereign is the one who decides when the law counts and when it doesn't, as well as what we do during the exceptional periods in which the law does not apply. Thus sovereignty is primarily the power to make decisions within a period of crisis or national emergency, when the law is suspended. Schmitt argues that this power is not just necessary in times of emergency or crisis, but is essential for establishing the law itself.

Discussing sovereignty's relationship to the normal structures of the law, Schmitt writes that "for a legal order to make sense, a normal situation must exist, and he is sovereign who definitely decides whether this normal situation actually exists."[4] Given that sovereignty is the power to decide when the law doesn't count, it follows that it is also the power to decide when the law does count, since the power to decide on the exception is also, logically, the power to decide on the norm. Sovereignty, thus, makes possible the founding of a legal and political order and is another name for the power exercised by the antagonism of the friend/enemy distinction, the sovereign will of the people. Now, as sovereignty is, for Schmitt, fundamentally aligned with the friend/enemy distinction, it would not be surprising if it suffered from the same kind of paradoxical structure.

"I Was Thinking Two Things, But Only Mean One of Them" — Guard

The power to make a decision, to choose one thing over another, to say I'll take this and not that, is the power of sovereignty. As Schmitt writes, "the decision on the exception [which is to say the power of sovereignty] is a decision in the truest sense."[5] Sovereignty is the power to decide what one will do outside of any rules or laws. This is not to say that one may not have reasons for one's decisions or a logic by which one decides between possible choices. But in the end, one must always choose whether to follow those rules or not. This lack of a governing rule is what makes sovereignty so hard to secure and justify, since, at the end of the day, there seems to be no way to adjudicate between competing sovereign claims.

How do we decide which decisions are right? When two people make opposing choices, how can we determine which is best? In fact, how could we know if any claim or decision is ever truly sovereign, legitimate, or binding? The problem here is that sovereignty leads to what philosophers call an infinite regress, every sovereign decision needing another sovereign decision to make its sovereignty legitimate, and then another, and another, into infinity. This problem of regress is just another way of talking about the paradox of the friend/enemy distinction, insofar as the expulsion of the enemy proves a contradictory and never-ending task. The detour through sovereignty shows that the problems raised by Schmitt are problems both for an individual notion of decision and responsibility and for state and political structures. In both cases, this logic poses fundamental problems for the possibility not just for legitimate decision making but also for responsibility.

The questions of decision and responsibility play a key role in the story and gameplay of *BioShock Infinite*. Anna becomes increasingly obsessed with whether she and Booker are responsible for the events unfolding around them. She wonders to what degree they are to blame for the violence and death they see everywhere. This worry is, however, complicated by their constant jumping through "tears" into alternative versions of Columbia, where even a small change in one reality may have massive effects in another. The problem that arises from these tears is that by splitting into multiple versions of themselves, it becomes difficult to know which version is the "real" one; that is, the one capable of being responsible for all the others. While this splitting is of course fictional, in *BioShock Infinite* it appears as the perfect metaphor for the infinite regress one sees in sovereignty—the search for a true, legitimate sovereign decision leading necessarily to an infinite multiplying of ultimately unjustifiable decisions. In the face of this conundrum, what can we possibly do? Or how can we ever know if we have made a justifiable decision?

Players are forced to make a number of decisions throughout *BioShock Infinite*, without any way of knowing what the outcomes of these decisions will be. The first is the choice of whether to throw a baseball at the couple on stage at the Raffle and the second is the choice of which necklace Anna should wear. It turns out that none of these decisions has any real impact on the game. In fact, the game seems to suggest that none of the decisions that Booker, Anna, or the player makes are of much consequence. This is true even of Booker's saving of Anna, which does nothing to eliminate the possibility of Comstock coming to power in one of the other "lighthouse" worlds. The game, in fact, offers only one solution to these problems, and it's a bleak one: the elimination of Booker DeWitt, and with him the very possibility of Comstock, Anna, and Columbia existing at all. The lesson of this ending seems to be that "you can't lose, if you don't play." Given the problems and paradoxes faced by the attempt to ground a legitimate democratic, secular state, one can perhaps relate to this pessimistic conclusion. Maybe the only solution is simply to give up on the possibility of legitimate power and politics altogether, accepting, in the end, that politics is nothing but the exercise of power, sometimes for good and sometimes for evil. And yet...

Bird or Cage?

In one of the coolest-looking and creepiest segments of the game, DeWitt is whisked through a tear to a Columbia in which he was unable to rescue Anna and she became Comstock's successor. In this world, Columbia attacks the "Sodom below" in order to exterminate the non-believers. This is the world in which Comstock's victory is utterly complete, where the hope for freedom and revolution has entirely failed. However, even in this world, there remains a possibility of thwarting Comstock. The Anna in this world is in every way a convert to Comstock's agenda, claiming to be unable to stop the massacre that she has put into motion. Yet it is she who opens the tear that allows Booker to return to his own time and, ultimately, to save Anna. Hence, perhaps the game's conclusion isn't as bleak as it seems. Maybe it's a problem of time and hindsight?

There's an interesting catch-22 in the choices that players are asked to make throughout *BioShock Infinite*. They are asked to choose between options that don't ultimately matter. Yet they can only discover this truth by making the choices and seeing what happens. Perhaps this is the subversive, revolutionary message of *BioShock Infinite*, the message that speaks to the possibility of legitimate political foundings and the questions raised by Carl Schmitt—namely, that we can't know if we have made legitimate choices or if we have the ability to challenge political oppression until we try.

Notes

1. Carl Schmitt, *The Concept of the Political*, trans. George Schwab (Chicago, IL: University of Chicago Press, 1996), 27.
2. Ibid.

3. Carl Schmitt, *Political Theology: Four Chapters on the Concept of Sovereignty*, trans. George Schwab (Cambridge, MA: MIT Press, 1985), 5.
4. Ibid., 13.
5. Ibid., 6.

11

Propaganda, Lies, and Bullshit in *BioShock*'s Rapture

Rachel McKinnon

From nearly our first experience entering the underwater city of Rapture in *BioShock*, we're treated to a taste of Andrew Ryan's propaganda in the form of the following message:

> I am Andrew Ryan, and I'm here to ask you a question. Is a man not entitled to the sweat of his brow? "No!" says the man in Washington, "it belongs to the poor." "No!" says the man in the Vatican, "it belongs to God." "No!" says the man in Moscow, "it belongs to everyone." I rejected those answers; instead, I chose something different. I chose the impossible. I chose... Rapture. A city where the artist would not fear the censor; where the scientist would not be bound by petty morality; where the great would not be constrained by the small! And with the sweat of your brow, Rapture can become your city as well.

This is part of Ryan's ideology, which closely follows Ayn Rand's (1905–82) Objectivism. It's the idea on which he designs Rapture and its laws, glorifying people who are producers and masters of their own fate and denigrating those Ryan refers to as "parasites" or slaves. Through propagandistic messages, he champions Objectivism, pictorially emblazoning it, for example, on placards in shopping carts along with the text: "Is a man not entitled to the sweat of his brow?"

But what is propaganda, and what makes it problematic? Are all instances of propaganda lies? Are all cases of propaganda morally problematic? Are all lies problematic? And finally, is there a difference between bullshit and propaganda?

BioShock and Philosophy: Irrational Game, Rational Book, First Edition. Edited by Luke Cuddy.
© 2015 John Wiley & Sons, Inc. Published 2015 by John Wiley & Sons, Inc.

"Even in the Book of Lies, Sometimes You Find Truth"—Andrew Ryan

"Is a man not entitled to the sweat of his brow?" Ryan's view is that one is entitled to the products of one's work, and *not* entitled to the products of another's work. He is committed to a view of capitalism where the rich deserve to be rich, through their own talent, intellect, and efforts, and the poor deserve to be poor, through their laziness and stupidity. It's a view that the ideal society is an extreme meritocracy: whatever one has in life is connected to one's merits. Not surprisingly, most of Ryan's propaganda messages revolve around reinforcing this ideology.

One commonplace view of propaganda is that it's a lie in the service of a government's goals. Some commentators suggest that the point of propaganda is to serve the interests of the propagandists themselves, to persuade people that there is only one valid perspective and to eliminate all others.[1]

So what difference is there between propaganda and lies? Contemporary philosopher Jennifer Saul provides a useful definition of lying.[2] Simplifying a little, a speaker lies if and only if she says something that she believes to be false. So in lying, a speaker misrepresents what she believes to be true. However, it's possible to lie and yet say something that happens to be true, provided that the speaker *believes* it to be false. This is an important part of the definition.

Andrew Ryan regularly says that citizens of Rapture need to avoid all contact with the surface world because it's filled with parasites who seek to destroy Rapture. Let's assume that Ryan doesn't actually believe this. It's quite possible Ryan merely thinks that there are values and objects on the surface world that he doesn't want to pollute Rapture's citizens. But let's also assume that the surface world has a real problem with the existence of Rapture, and that it really is filled with people who want to see Rapture fall. Even though what Ryan says about the outside world is true, he's lying because he believes it to be false. As Ryan says, "Even in the book of lies, sometimes you find truth."

When we lie, we want our hearer to think that we're trying to say something true. That's how lies work, after all: I trust that you're trying to tell me something true. When a person lies, they perform what we call a *speech act*. Different speech acts include things like questions, commands, assertions, requests, promises, and so on. Lies involve assertions, claims that something is true. Good liars, then, assert something that they believe to be false, but that the hearer thinks the speaker believes to be true. We recognize that the speaker at least *appears* to be trying to say something true. This is different from what contemporary philosopher Harry Frankfurt calls "bullshit."[3]

That's Bullshit!

When we lie, we say something that we believe to be false. This means that what a liar says is somewhat connected to the way things are, since liars are aiming to say something that isn't true. According to Harry Frankfurt, though, bullshit is when the speaker doesn't particularly care whether what she says is true or false. The bullshitter is up to something different. Whereas the liar is trying to misrepresent the way things are and what he believes to be true, the bullshitter is trying to misrepresent what she's up to with her assertion. The liar only succeeds if we incorrectly believe that he believes what he says ("Any contact with the surface exposes Rapture to the very parasites we fled from," Ryan says in an audio diary). The liar has to convince us that he's at least trying to say something that he believes to be true. However, the bullshitter succeeds when we incorrectly believe that she is even *trying* to say something that she believes to be true. Frankly, the bullshitter doesn't care whether what she says is true or false; that's beside the point. So what the bullshitter says is completely disconnected from what she takes to be the truth.

This analysis suggests that propaganda is more closely connected to bullshitting than lying. When Ryan says, "Any contact with the surface exposes Rapture to the very parasites we fled from," he doesn't care whether it's true or false. He's just trying to influence his citizens' reactions to smugglers, which is of course connected to his move to institute the death penalty for smugglers. Now, certainly, sometimes propaganda involves lies, when speakers (or the government) are trying to say something they believe to be false. But if saying something true would work just as well, maybe even better, they might just as well speak the truth. What matters isn't fooling citizens about what's true or false; what matters is *controlling* the citizens' thoughts and behaviors so as to further the government's needs. Whoever, or whatever, is using the propaganda is trying to make it appear as though they care about (saying) what's true. But they don't care, not really. So what they say is driven by what will work, not what's true or false. What liars say is driven by what they think is false. Propaganda, then, is more closely associated with bullshit than lying.

Frankfurt also argues that bullshit is more morally problematic than lying. Skilled liars also have to be skilled at discerning the truth so that they can aim to avoid it in what they say. Frankfurt thus thinks that frequent liars won't lose their ability to discern truth. But skilled bullshitters don't have to have any skill at discerning the truth, since they don't care about whether what they say is true or false. And Frankfurt suggests that habitual bullshitters will *lose* (or lessen) their ability to discern the truth. So he suggests that bullshit is a bigger enemy of truth than lies.

If I'm right that propaganda is more closely associated with bullshit than lies, then this also means that we should be particularly worried by governments (or individuals with power, such as Andrew Ryan) that engage in lots of propaganda. One worry is that these governments may attenuate or even lose their ability to determine what's true. Andrew Ryan may have done just that. In a later audio diary recording we find in the first game, he says the following:

> Could I have made mistakes? One does not build cities if one is guided by doubt. But can one govern in absolute certainty? I know that my beliefs have elevated me, just as I know that the things I have rejected would have destroyed me. But the city… it is collapsing before my… have I become so convinced by my own beliefs that I have stopped seeing the truth? Perhaps. But Atlas is out there, and he aims to destroy me, and destroy my city. To question is to surrender. I will not question.

He admits that he may have convinced himself of his own propaganda, to the point where he can't easily determine what's true and what's false. If propaganda were more like lies, then one could simply disbelieve one's propaganda to get at the truth. But what makes propaganda so troubling is that it's more like bullshit: it's hard to tell whether it's true or false. And after engaging in enough of it, even the government may lose the ability to tell the difference.

Noble Lies, Noble Propaganda

Can a government or speaker be warranted or justified in their use of propaganda? We can answer this by considering what makes some lies good, and what makes others bad. This is a debate in philosophy known as the "norms of assertion." In this debate, norms are standards for evaluating actions. So if one violates a norm of assertion, then one did something wrong. A natural intuition is that all lies are bad: they're unwarranted assertions. But I don't think that's right.

Near the end of the game, as Jack (the player) works to confront Ryan, we hear Ryan say:

> So far away from your family, from your friends, from everything you ever loved. But, for some reason you like it here. You feel something you can't quite put your finger on. Think about it for a second and maybe the word will come to you: nostalgia.

Of course, Jack has no family or friends, at least not the ones he thinks he remembers (since they're a fiction planted in his memory). So Ryan's lie here is really in service of having Jack come to realize that he's just a pawn—Fontaine's pawn, for Fontaine (who is also known as Atlas) purchased Jack's embryo in order to cultivate Jack as a tool to take down Ryan for the control of Rapture. Indeed, Ryan ends up telling Jack the truth when Jack finally confronts Ryan face to face (and Ryan eventually orders Jack to kill Ryan).

I've argued elsewhere that some lies are warranted, provided that the lie is in service of the hearer (potentially) coming to know the truth.[4] That's what's going on with Ryan's lie about Jack's family and loved ones. Jack isn't actually far away from the people he knows (or used to know before his memory was altered): he was created and raised in Rapture. However, by connecting Jack's sense of being far from the people he knows, and yet probably also having a sense of nostalgia or familiarity with Rapture, Ryan is trying to get Jack to come to know the truth about who, and what, he is. Of course, Ryan is also doing this to try to control Jack and stop Fontaine's takeover, but that's beside the point.

So while what Ryan says to Jack is false, and he knows it to be false, he tells *that* lie only in order for Jack eventually to learn about the truth. So while his assertion is "proximally" false (what he says is literally false), he says it in service of a related truth. On my view, when we assert properly, aiming at saying something true, our assertion is warranted. This means that some false assertions – even ones we know to be false – may be warranted if that proper aim is in place. And this is what happens with this lie of Ryan's, making it a warranted lie. Of course, *many* of Ryan's lies don't have this structure, and so are problematic.

On this concept of warranted assertion, then, not all lies are bad. Lies in service of the truth are warranted. Earlier, I argued that propaganda is more closely associated with bullshit than lies. Lies, remember, involve speakers saying something that they believe is false. Bullshit involves speakers saying something and not caring whether what they say is true or false. Now, while one might not strictly care whether what one says is true or false when one bullshits, one might bullshit with a further aim of truth in mind. Suppose that Andrew Ryan is right that smugglers' contact with the outside world will expose Rapture to a number of problems that he's trying to protect the citizens against, yet he knows that, strictly speaking, it's false that "Any contact with the surface exposes Rapture to the very parasites we fled from." Still, he doesn't say this because he wants to fool them about the truth, per se; he does it to control their behavior and their opinions of the smugglers. It's propaganda. We may suppose, though, that he does it for his citizens' own good. He uses this propaganda in order for his citizens to see something that (we may suppose) is true: the smugglers *will* expose Rapture's citizens to the very problems of the outside world that Ryan is trying to protect them from.

Propaganda that proximally doesn't aim at truth (or falsity) but does have a more distant aim of having hearers come to believe something true seems sufficiently close to the "good" lie that Ryan tells Jack. Both are quite plausibly warranted assertions. If that's right, then not all propaganda counts as unwarranted assertions, and not all propaganda is clearly morally problematic. However, Frankfurt's concern still stands: those who engage in too much propaganda may attenuate or lose their ability to tell the difference between truth and falsity. As Atlas (Frank Fontaine) says: "Ryan and his precious Rapture. You don't have to build a city to make people worship you... just make the chumps believe they're worth a nickel."

Notes

1. Nicholas Cull, David Culbert, and David Welch, *Propaganda and Mass Persuasion: A Historical Encyclopedia, 1500 to the Present* (Santa Barbara, CA: ABC-CLIO, 2003).

2. Jennifer Saul, *Lying, Misleading, and What Is Said: An Exploration in Philosophy of Language and Ethics* (Oxford: Oxford University Press, 2012).

3. Harry Frankfurt, "On Bullshit," in *The Importance of What We Care About* (Cambridge: Cambridge University Press, 1988), 117–133.

4. Rachel McKinnon, "The Supportive Reasons Norm of Assertion," *American Philosophical Quarterly* 50 (2013): 121–135.

12

The Vox Populi Group, Marx, and Equal Rights for All

Tyler DeHaven and Chris Hendrickson

To call Comstock's regime in *BioShock Infinite* oppressive, some people would argue, is an understatement. In fact, a modern interpretation of Karl Marx's (1818–83) *Manifesto of the Communist Party* can help to explain how that regime uses religion, industrialization, and government soldiers to oppress and subvert the labor class. Comstock's empire acts as an enforcer of the status quo, which the ruling elite benefits from. But oppression, it seems, is not limited to the ruling class. The story of the Vox Populi embodies conflict theory—one popular interpretation of Marx's ideas—portraying a bloody revolution that loses sight of its ideals, turns anarchistic, and becomes the new oppressor.

Marxism and Class Warfare: The Bourgeoisie Oppresses the Proletariat

At the core of Marxist thought is conflict or struggle. More specifically, Marx saw history as a constant struggle for power between classes of people over the material means of production, including transportation technology, weapons, and food. But non-material powers are also at play, including human rights, class privileges, and self-determination. The conflict itself occurs between the upper class, or the bourgeoisie, and the lower class, or the proletariat.

BioShock and Philosophy: Irrational Game, Rational Book, First Edition. Edited by Luke Cuddy.
© 2015 John Wiley & Sons, Inc. Published 2015 by John Wiley & Sons, Inc.

The bourgeoisie enjoys status and privilege as society's elite, gaining this advantage through the effective use of trade and industry. In Columbia, Zachary Hale Comstock and Jeremiah Fink illustrate the way the bourgeoisie may come to create and control the means of production: these men respectively develop and enforce the system by which the rest of the city lives. Comstock's "prophecy" creates a group of beliefs and moral codes that inform the lives of his citizens. For example, Comstock relays some of his "prophetic" vision by stating, "No animal is born free, except the white man. And it is our burden to care for the rest of creation." The industrialist Fink echoes this sentiment in stating, "Well, I've a man in Georgia who'll lease us as many Negro convicts as you can board! Why, you can say they're simple souls, in penance for rising above their station." Thus, Columbia adopts Comstock and Fink's prejudices as legitimate social standards.

Further, the bourgeoisie enjoys a disproportionate amount of wealth that accumulates because of the entire society's labor. As a matter of law, Comstock requires that the city donate 50 percent of its profits to him as a personal tithe. Due to its control over the labor and trade of society, the bourgeoisie contentedly profits from the current system, with no desire to change it.

However, members of the much larger and poorer class, the proletariat, certainly lack the advantages of the bourgeoisie. Shantytown, home to Columbia's working-class people, exhibits the poverty of the lower class. Their squalid, rickety homes offer little protection from the elements, and some of the residents resort to washing their clothes in the rain gutter. While the proletariat's labor produces a great deal of material wealth, the proletariat rarely sees the bulk of the profit— the bourgeoisie grabs it. Lacking other options, the proletariat must participate in the labor system that unfairly exploits its work, which steadily increases the workers' resentment. Naturally, this tension cannot build indefinitely without release.

Proletariat Suppression through Propaganda, Inequality, and Control

To perpetuate its currently advantageous system, the ruling class oppresses the labor class through control and the exercise of power. In *BioShock Infinite*, Comstock and Fink keep the working class enslaved through several institutions, including religion, government, and industry. Comstock established Columbia with a prophetic, Christian faith in which he reigns as the divinely favored leader with the gift of seeing the future. There is also a patriotic civil religion, an "opiate of the masses," in which George Washington, Thomas Jefferson, and Benjamin Franklin are worshiped as representations of law, morality, and science. Comstock encourages this blind patriotism and glorifies himself in historical exhibits at the Hall of Heroes and the creation of Soldier's Field. In Lutece's words, these attractions are "themed to acquaint children with national service," perpetuating the class divisions into the next generation.

The bourgeoisie uses public institutions to subvert any radical actions by the proletariat and to protect its accumulation of power. Indeed, Columbia Security is Comstock's means to eliminate any threat to the bourgeoisie, most notably the Vox Populi. The Word of the Prophet kinetoscopes, radio announcements, and the Annual Raffle and Fair serve as anti-Vox propaganda for the Columbian populace. Before the Vox ever show up they are gossiped about by fearful citizens in hushed whispers. When Booker is publicly identified by Fink as Comstock's prophesied "False Shepherd," Columbia Security is quick to step in as the enforcer of the status quo.

In order to stay in power, the bourgeoisie must control the means of production. The bourgeoisie creates pauperism among the proletariat, and Fink exploits the labor class with the terms of employment at his factory. Shantytown is the home of the lower class, and where Daisy Fitzroy began inciting the Vox Populi to revolt against the upper class. It resembles a Hooverville of the 1920s—tin-roofed shacks, old mattresses, and refuse abound. The Handyman is the literal example of the proletariat condition: any worker who is grievously injured on the job can be recreated as a mechanical work slave, thus able to continue serving Fink Industries.

As the friction builds between the bourgeoisie and the proletariat, historical processes contribute to the inevitable collapse of capitalism. The collapse is not the "realization of a moral ideal," but rather the result of processes that set in motion dramatic societal changes. In *BioShock Infinite*, the simmering friction between the upper and lower classes boils over into the rise of the Vox Populi. Though the Vox are incited to action through Daisy Fitzroy's call to arms, Columbia's societal shift is a result of the Vox's historic revolution, with little thought given to any morality besides self-preservation and revenge.

Conflict theory, a modern sociological interpretation of Marxist theory, views class power struggles as a necessary condition of history. Conflict theorists note that unequal bourgeoisie and proletariat groups usually have conflicting values and agendas, which compete against each other. This constant competition between groups forms the basis for the ever-changing nature of society.

Early in the game, Booker passes through a home that is actually the secret headquarters for the Columbia Friends of the Negro Society. Flyers plastered around the room read: "Until the Negro Is Equal None of Us Are Equal." Later on, Booker discovers an exclusive secret society, known as the Fraternal Order of the Raven. Its projectors display "Comstock Phrenological Study" slides with images of Native Americans and the human brain divided up into areas for character traits. The pseudo-science of phrenology involves the use of cranial measurements to determine personality traits—often confirming the "native brutality" or "criminal urges" of minorities while emphasizing the superiority of Caucasians. Thus we see the racism that Columbia's elite embraces. These two contrasting groups within Columbia illustrate competing class ideologies with regard to racial equality. While conflict theory emphasizes the competitive nature of factions within society, another perspective explains how social institutions coexist and thereby achieve societal stability.

Functionalism: We Are Parts of the Whole

Multiple social groups emerge throughout the story of *BioShock Infinite* with competing ideologies: their own interpretations of what is "best" for all. The lens of structural functionalism, pioneered by Herbert Spencer in *Principles of Sociology*, views the answer as a complex system, where society's parts evolve and work together to grow more stable. Social structures and elements such as norms, customs, traditions, and institutions have specific functions that work together cohesively, promoting the overall good of society. As one observes the people of Columbia, several classes and members of society are revealed, each playing a role in keeping the whole society together.

Though the city's separate institutions and classes operate with independent goals, the sum of their actions stabilizes Columbia as a system. A working class under Fink grants Columbia an infrastructure, Comstock's enthusiastic vision and religion rally everyone behind a unified cause, and Lutece supplies the technological breakthroughs necessary to create such innovations as prophecy, interdimensional travel, and a flying city. Columbia Security's unquestioning service under Comstock provides a classic example of a military dictatorship, while Fink's working class is ultimately the supporting backbone of Columbia. The upper-class citizens benefit from the working class's labors, and the reminders to stay wary of the Vox Populi function as a means to motivate and reinforce the upper class's inherent mistrust of the working class, and also to affirm its status as the privileged class. Racial classism is also demonstrated by the Columbia Friends of the Negro Society, the Order of the Raven, Slate's revolution, and Daisy Fitzroy's Vox Populi. Each of these institutions functions to promote its radical views within Columbia.

Fink takes a functionalist perspective on society, in which he and Comstock are lions who rule and keep order among the lesser creatures. Members of the working class are viewed as cattle who labor for the rest of Columbia. The Vox Populi are hyenas who steal from the lions and profit from the work of the cattle. Casting himself as a protective lion, Fink provides food, clothing, shelter, and medicine for the working class. His comment that "only an anarchist would want workers' comp, paid vacations, and 8-hour workdays" illustrates the functionalist perspective of stability—that it perpetuates the status quo, a system of exploitation that works to serve the city. Under this theory, each institution and class provides the structure needed for society to continue existing and evolving. Religion provides such a supporting structure as the shepherd's staff that herds the sheep and cattle of Columbia.

Comstock uses various religious notions to justify the foundation and structure of Columbian society. For example, when describing his "divine inspiration" for the floating city, Comstock states, "And when the Angel Columbia gave unto the Founders the tools to build the new Eden, they did so without hesitation. For 85 years, they prepared the way of the Lord..." This "vision" introduces Columbia's state religion, which deifies the American Founding Fathers. Immediately on his arrival in the city, Booker discovers three large statues built in the likenesses of George Washington, Thomas Jefferson, and Benjamin Franklin. Worshipers mill around the "Welcome Center" while offering prayers to Washington for strength, to Jefferson for wisdom, and to Franklin for justice. They end their prayers with the invocation: "In the name of the sword, the scroll, and the key: amen." Such invocations directly relate to the Founders and the civil religion of Columbia: the sword for Washington, the scroll for Jefferson, and the key for Franklin. And, as part of this state religion, stories abound of the Founders' noble exploits. In Columbia, Washington is depicted as crossing the Delaware with an angel's flaming sword in hand. History itself, then, proves malleable for the sake of emphasizing Columbia's superiority. Surely, if God commands that the city's structure and foundation should occur as Comstock relates, then the populace must accept it. Religion in Columbia necessarily functions to reassure its citizens that they should not complain about their roles or question the roles of others.

Comstock uses religious references to delude his followers and legitimize his authority. He relates that the angel named Columbia granted him a vision of the city's foundation precisely because he was formerly sinful and that made him all the more worthy of grace. However, Comstock never actually spoke to an angel. Rather, Lutece describes in a Voxophone how Comstock looked into her machine and saw "a window not into prophecy, but probability." Clearly, no angels revealed the proper future to him: he embellished his story in order to become a prophet, and thus Columbia's uncontested leader. Lutece's contraption figuratively became the angel Columbia. Despite all of his fervent bandstanding, Comstock is nothing more than a fraud.

Ironically, Comstock uses his contrived "prophecy" to demonize his ultimate enemy as the False Shepherd. Rather quickly after his arrival in Columbia, Booker finds that he is in fact this prophesied enemy. Unlike Comstock, though, Booker makes no religious claims whatsoever. In further contrast to Comstock, he abandons any attempts to deceive Elizabeth, whom Comstock calls "the Lamb." Though initially deceptive, Booker eventually chooses to follow Elizabeth and to protect her as she independently acts on her desires. The "Prophet Comstock," on the other hand, seeks to control and to use her abilities to incinerate New York City, which he colorfully characterizes as the "Sodom Below." In these many ways, Comstock uses religion to establish and maintain a system that he and the others in the elite benefit from. The agnostic Booker's arrival and subsequent journey set in motion escalating events, causing that religiously motivated deception to fall apart and the entire system to transform.

The functionalist perspective often casts religion as a social structure that keeps society together despite any negative costs it may have for any particular group. The Rawlsian Difference Principle, on the other hand—which is spelled out in philosopher John Rawls' (1921–2002) seminal book *A Theory of Justice*—is a counter-utilitarian argument that says that any differences in wealth must ultimately be to the benefit of the least well advantaged. A Rawlsian would argue that the Founders had no right to subject the lower class to such squalid working and living conditions just so that the privileged Columbian citizens could profit. Everyone must profit from the inequality in some way, or else equality must prevail as the fairest approach to justice.

A functionalist could consider the Rawlsian viewpoint as selfish, and regard the Vox Populi as egotistical, ignorant, and self-interested. The rise of the Vox could be viewed as undermining their responsibility to their city, to the detriment of Columbia's economic and social stability. One must consider what the society as a whole would be like if the working class or the Vox get their way, versus the stability of the current social infrastructure. Would Columbia ultimately profit or suffer under Vox Populi majority rule? As Booker faces off in a final showdown against the full strength of the Vox Populi, the reality of Columbia burning, filled with so many dead, and dominated by the savage Vox is a chaotic nightmare. Does this cast the goals of the oppressed working class and the Vox Populi revolution as ultimately selfish? Columbia is arguably worse off at the game's end than when ruled by Comstock's comparatively peaceful regime.

Symbolism: How We Create Meaning

By observing the symbols in *BioShock Infinite*, we can start to interpret and understand the motivations of institutions and individuals. Comstock's religion, Columbian media, and Fink Industries are the critical institutions whose influences on the people of Columbia inform the power struggles between classes.

BioShock Infinite exemplifies the manner in which societies often poach Christian imagery to promote an agenda or to deceive the masses. The game's primary villain, Comstock, uses religious symbolism to endow his prejudices with a kind of divine approval. As he states:

> And when I came to Washington, there were few in Congress who saw my vision for Columbia. But it is the burden of the Prophet to bring the wicked to righteousness. For what am I, if not a mirror to reflect the face of God?

Confident in his plan for the city, Comstock takes up the role of "prophet" and uses his uncanny foresight to establish a city whose moral codes and social rules reflect his biases. In speaking of great American leaders, the prophet decries Lincoln, saying, "when the Great Apostate came, he brought war with him, and the fields of Eden [America] were soaked with the blood of brothers. The only emancipation he brought was death." The prophet again invokes religion to promote his personal beliefs, going so far as to cast Lincoln out of Christian society because of his support of African Americans' freedom. Comstock's racist manipulation of Christian belief systems is further reflected in his rule of the city when he states:

> To tax the black more than the white, is that not cruel? To forbid the mixing of the races, is that not cruel? To give the vote to the white man, and deny it to the yellow, the black, the red—is that not cruel? Hm. But is it not cruel to banish your children from a perfect garden? Or drown your flock under an ocean of water? Cruelty can be instructive, and what is Columbia, if not the schoolhouse of the Lord?

As prophet and ruler, Comstock presumably speaks with a divine imperative, and so the people follow him on the basis of their religious faith.

However, as the other original Founders of Columbia understand, Comstock is no true prophet. His religious fervor merely serves as a convenient tool for the deception of his "flock." Fink, the head of Columbia's industrial sector, reflects that "belief ... is just a commodity. And old Comstock, well he does produce. But, like any tradesman, he's obliged to barter his product for the earthly one." Comstock's religion proves no more holy than snake oil and Columbia's people buy it without question. Since the source of the Prophet's visions is a machine created by the

Luteces, there is no divinity involved; Comstock's prophecies are entirely man-made. Nearly all of the Christian symbolism in Columbia extends from Comstock's schemes, which promote *his* version of the Truth. In this way, the state religion that Comstock establishes maintains a class division based on bourgeois prejudices and his personal agenda.

Years before Columbia was raised to the skies, Comstock had burnt some Native Americans alive to prove that he felt no kinship with them despite sharing their skin color. He could not tolerate his captain's goading: "Your family tree shelters a teepee or two, doesn't it, son?" The prophet's awful, desperate measure attests to both horribly racist attitudes and an utter lack of remorse or ownership—such deeds belonged to another man now washed away by the waters of baptism. He describes baptism as a process in which "One man goes in the waters of baptism. A different man comes out, born again..." After baptism, then, Comstock need not account for the atrocious deeds he committed in the past, nor even remember them. With his past drowned in the baptismal waters, the "redeemed prophet" is now freed to commit similar atrocities in the future.

Immediately on entering Columbia, Booker DeWitt discovers his identity as the False Shepherd. According to Comstock, "the False Shepherd is coming to lead my Lamb astray." The Lamb is Elizabeth, the very girl Booker seeks to rescue because of an unknown benefactor's promise to "wipe away his debt." Elizabeth's prophesied destiny is to destroy the "Sodom Below" and thus fulfill Comstock's grand designs. Due to Booker's interference, though, she escapes the confines of the prophet's plans and eventually pursues her own path. In this way, Booker proves a striking foil to Comstock in that he eventually enables Elizabeth to gain freedom.

Strikingly, Booker rejects the very interpretation of baptism that Comstock finds most appealing: he doesn't believe that his notorious past can be washed away. In fact, one of the game's first scenes depicts Booker scoffing at the idea of "washing away sin," and he later tells Elizabeth that one can *at best* learn to live with the past. Unlike the Prophet, who uses baptism to "wipe away his sin," the False Shepherd ultimately comes to terms with his past and makes a choice to "square his debt." Booker ironically accepts a life-ending baptism by Elizabeth's hand after he understands that the only way to destroy Comstock in all realities is to sacrifice himself.

In a larger sense, Booker's arrival proves the catalyst for the destruction of Comstock's regime. He saves Elizabeth from Comstock's manipulation, arms the Vox Populi, and ultimately kills Comstock with his bare hands. Therefore, Booker destroys the very fabrications that enabled Comstock's manipulations of Columbia. In the sociological sense, Booker's defiance of Comstock enables the Vox Revolution to evolve from a grassroots movement into an influential institution that stands for social change in the face of the bourgeoisie's religious oppression.

Columbian media reinforces class division by casting anyone sympathetic to a potentially rebellious proletariat as suspicious. It even goes so far as to demonize the Vox Populi by making obviously contrived associations between them and ruin. For example:

> Shortly after 1 o'clock this afternoon, the scoundrel—believed by many to be Vox Populi—began his terrible rampage ... Trouble began almost instantly. Full of wrath, and bent on harm, the Anarchist maliciously wounded several Columbian Peacemakers—before then arming himself and firing into an assemblage of virtuous fair-goers.

Though Booker never had any connection to the Vox, the media eagerly attributes his violence to them. Further, the media impresses such a strong fear of the Vox into the populace that it cautions them to look for murderous rebels at all times. The media even provides methods for exposing such agents, like:

> Is your housekeeper acting suspicious? Try asking the girl a few questions, such as "Don't you think those Vox Populi folk have a valid complaint against the Prophet?" And "I'm sure some of your friends have attended meetings... I'd sure like to see what they're all about." Now, back to the music...

The Word of the Prophet kinetoscopes are another example of propaganda and indoctrination. The kinetoscope entitled "Solving the Irish Problem!" casts this social group as drunks, brood mares, and future recruits of the Vox Populi: "Send them to Finkton ... They'll work, or by God, die trying!" Clearly, then, Columbia's media seeks to convert the disenfranchised lower class into cogs for the machine that is Columbia's means of production, further empowering the Founders.

Columbia's industrialization is represented by Fink's production empire, which is responsible for nearly every piece of mechanical infrastructure in the city. Floating buildings, blimps, airships, skylines, weaponry, vending machines, and Vigors are all mass-produced at Fink Industries. Fink and the Founders know that owning the means of production is critical to the success and stability of Columbia, and thus they are encouraged to protect the status quo and their own prosperity. Comstock utilizes Finkton to create his own personal army for simultaneously protecting and assuring his control of his city. Daisy Fitzroy, advocating for the proletariat, sees Fink Industries as an institution of degradation and enslavement. The Vox Populi fight to repurpose this institution for their own advantage in the war against the Founders. Industrialization in Columbia is responsible for Comstock's army, Fitzroy's bitter enemies, and Booker's main obstacles: Columbia security, the Handyman, and Songbird.

When Booker explores Columbia Security, the player can observe signage around the station that reads: "Protecting our Faith, Wealth, and Racial Purity." This meme demonstrates the upper class's values, and the rationale behind keeping the working class impoverished. Outfitted with Fink-made weaponry and loyal to Comstock, the player views this institution as a formidable obstacle to be overcome. The Handyman, introduced as a marvel of Fink Industries, represents to the citizenry a new feat of uniquely Columbian ingenuity. To the player, the Handyman presents an escalated challenge and makes tactical gameplay necessary. Songbird is Comstock's pet and security measure, while to Elizabeth it is a protector, jailer, and her only friend. The player sees this boss character as a nearly insurmountable "Game Over" whose changing eye color serves as an instructional cue, letting the player know if Songbird is friendly, aware but indifferent, or openly hostile.

In order for the bourgeoisie to own the means of production and keep the working class oppressed, it uses propaganda and indoctrination as powerful agents of control. Fink Industries uses visual and audio indoctrination to design and instill a culture of servitude into the lower class. This enables the continuation of both Columbia's industry and the luxuries the Founders enjoy.

The signage, background music, and Fink's recorded audio loop within Finkton exemplify how the Founders create the conditions necessary for workforce enslavement and owning the means of production. As with many areas of the game, the signage in Finkton elaborates on the values impressed on the workforce by the institution. The signs and posters on the walls read:

- "A Good Worker Always has his eyes on the task at hand!"
- "Eyes Forward!"
- "Your Family's Future Begins Today!"
- "Your Future Is Finkton"
- "Leaving Early? Watching the clock opens the door for others To Take Your Job!"
- "Killing Time Kills Columbia"

The player can also see a statue of a man and his family, with a plaque that reads "Fink is your Future" at the factory's Welcome Center. The music constantly playing to the metronome of a hammer knocking against wood subconsciously instills an unceasing, driving rhythm into the workers. Fink's propaganda audio loop uses animals as a metaphor to sell Fink's functionalist perspective. In metaphorically relating each group of Columbian society to animals as part of an overall ecology, Fink cajoles the workforce to willingly accept their lot in life:

> The most common complaint I hear from the working man is that they are ... unhappy ... with their lot. "Why torment yourself?" I ask. The ox cannot become a lion. And why would you want to? Who wants all those responsibilities and worry? You do your job, you eat your food, you go to sleep. Simplicity is beauty.

Further animal analogies from Fink portray the Vox as hyenas who offer nothing substantial, whereas Fink offers work that improves everyone's lives. Yet, Fink only provides survival-level needs to some of the lower class, and what should be paid to the workers as fair wages is reaped as pure profit for the upper-class citizenry. To the lower class of Columbia, following Fink's rules is the only way to survive. However, Fitzroy convinces the lower class that these conditions set by the Founders are oppressive and unacceptable:

> The Founders' belief is that we ain't no better than oxen. Think on that. Think on a man looking at you—your children—and seeing a beast

meant to be ruled over. Not someone capable of rational thought. Not someone with their own dreams and aspirations. Not someone trying to make sure their kids have it better than they did. The Founders see you as something to be controlled. To be told when to eat. When to sleep. When to stand and sit down. To say, "Yes sir," "No sir," "May I go to the bathroom, sir?" You ain't a person to them. You're a tool!

BioShock Infinite offers a compelling model of class struggle and how it affects the populace. On entering Columbia, the player may gaze around in awe at the majesty of a city in the clouds. However, as the story progresses, the harsh realities of Columbia are seen: it is built on a network of inequality and exploitation. Columbia's proletariat, the Vox Populi, enact a brutal revolution that leaves devastation in its wake. As Marx predicted, systems of prolonged inequality cannot last. The Vox Populi won their rights by destroying Columbia's former government and re-appropriating the means of production. *BioShock Infinite* depicts an oppressed class that, in its uprising, loses sight of its ideals, turns anarchistic, and becomes the new oppressor.

Part IV
THE CIRCUS OF VALUES

13

Infinite Lighthouses, Infinite Stories
BioShock and the Aesthetics of Video Game Storytelling

László Kajtár

"Infinite possibilities"—it's like the empty slogan of a laptop manufacturer or sports brand. It says nothing, because our lives often seem quite linear. Considering all the possibilities, all the things that you could have done or been, there is a certain melancholy to this human condition. This is one of the reasons why we like fiction so much—that is, imaginary stories in which we inhabit different people, viewpoints, and worlds. *BioShock Infinite* is a piece of fiction that lets you peer into a world where this linearity seems overridden by a multiverse where all the possibilities exist. Indeed, the storytelling in *Infinite* is a form of art.

"Not Stars, They're Doors"—Elizabeth

Wooden planks appear in front of you as you walk through an infinite ocean of lighthouses. At first, the ending of *BioShock Infinite* might seem like madness, but there's definitely a method in it. Ken Levine, formerly the creative director of Irrational Games and the creator of *BioShock*, thinks about stories. In an interview with gaming site Polygon, Levine shared a thought experiment that's been occupying him about "narrative legos," about creating an interactive story out of basic story elements.[1] So if a guy who thinks about these things is the

BioShock and Philosophy: Irrational Game, Rational Book, First Edition. Edited by Luke Cuddy.
© 2015 John Wiley & Sons, Inc. Published 2015 by John Wiley & Sons, Inc.

creative director for a game, you know that the game's story is going to make sense on some level.

Storytelling is important, maybe even more than many of us would think. Consider the religious zeal of Comstock, which led him to baptize Columbia the "New Eden." Comstock knows about the power of stories, and he based his creation of Columbia on a twisting and applying biblical and historical narratives. He dreamed up the myth of "The Lamb of Columbia," a story of how Elizabeth is savior or messiah of the floating city. This story is the reason behind the whole of Columbia turning against Booker, when he's discovered after the Ruffle and named as the "False Shepherd". The ancient Greek philosopher Plato (428/427–348/347 BCE) was aware of the power of stories too. Unlike Comstock, however, he didn't use them to support religious tyranny. Plato wrote dialogues in which characters debate and discuss philosophical matters, like what justice or virtue is, or how to live a good life. But sometimes Plato's characters discuss myths. These myths are related to the philosophical issue, but they illustrate or establish a point by telling a story of gods and heroes that the Greeks were fond of. Even in Plato's time, stories seemed uniquely important.

If you think about it, stories are unique in their potential to convey information in an effective way, to kick-start the engine in your brain, to affect you emotionally. Ideologies benefit from this. In *Infinite*, Comstock employs the power of rewriting the stories of history to support his fascist-xenophobic regime. The people of Columbia enthusiastically support white supremacy because a religious leader offers them a narrative about how America's fate depends on it. So because of their power, stories have these dangers. But why do they have this power? The literary scholar Jonathan Gottschall argues that humans are actually "wired" for storytelling.[2] As Gottschall says, in fiction we rehearse or simulate "troublesome" situations, which might assist in developing our abilities to cope. Speaking of coping, recall the line from Robert Lutece: "The mind of the subject will desperately struggle to create memories where none exist." One possible explanation for why the mind struggles to create memories is that the mind needs the memories to be part of a coherent story to help us make sense of ourselves and the world. The whole backstory of Booker about the debt and the girl is a coping mechanism for the disruptions caused by traveling through parallel realities.

Stories are important for video games.[3] Its story is one of the reasons *BioShock Infinite* resonates with audiences all around the world. During the combat sequences, you struggle to beat the enemies, to stay alive and to be able to shoot, burn, blow up, and electrocute Motorized Patriots or Handymen. You have an interactive stake in the game. It's not like a movie that you can just watch; you have to skillfully act to progress. Both Rapture and Columbia are among the most memorable video-game settings of all time. Because these environments are so well designed, the player gets quickly invested in the game. Typically, the player doesn't merely want to kill a bunch of enemies (there are games with better combat anyway), but wants to explore the world. When you wander off from the main storyline to investigate a building or listen to another Voxophone, you're not playing the game to beat it.[4] You're playing it because you are immersed in the world and the story. *BioShock Infinite* is thus a good example of why we can call some video games art.

The field of philosophy that deals with art is called aesthetics. It's notoriously difficult to give a definition of art. Why would you categorize a painting by Paul Cézanne under the same label as a postmodern dance performance or a Bauhaus building or an avant-garde poem? No matter how you try to capture the essential quality or qualities of art, there'll always be counter-examples. Such is the nature of human creativity. Putting these difficulties to the side, we'll focus on one philosopher, an American pragmatist named John Dewey (1859–1952). Most people, if asked to give examples of art, would list particular novels, poems, paintings, or symphonies. Dewey thought about art differently. He thought that art is not merely about objects but about experiences.[5] It's not just about the painting but also about seeing the painting. It's not just about the text of a poem but also about reading it. And this makes sense when it comes to video games like *BioShock Infinite*.

If you think that it's even worth asking the question of whether *BioShock Infinite* is art or not, then you might want to consider this: What is it we're asking about in this case? We're not asking about objects like the DVD or the files and folders. We're not curious about the strings of 1s and 0s that make up the code. When we ask whether *Infinite* is art, we're asking about the experience of playing it. To use a technical term, we're asking whether the experience is an "aesthetic" experience. We're asking whether the video game designers and programmers have managed to create something that can be enjoyed aesthetically.

For Dewey, the experience of art is not totally different from everyday experiences. Art doesn't belong in an alien realm. When you fill Booker's shoes, you can relate to him. He's motivated to get out of debt, so he goes on a seemingly typical "damsel in distress" mission. As the story develops, the emotional force gets stronger, and it's not about debt any more but about the sins of a father, about regrets and guilt and about establishing a connection to Elizabeth. In a sense, you virtually become Booker. You live through the beginning, middle, and end of *Infinite*'s story. From the Luteces dropping you off at the lighthouse to picking Anna up from her crib, you experience the narrative as an organic unity. At the end, you might even use Dewey's expression "that was *an* experience." The adventure through Columbia and parallel realities is not just an experience among others, it's *an* experience that is unique. For Dewey, this would be a sign of an aesthetic experience.[6] Playing through *BioShock Infinite* is an experience that is meaningful in a unitary and complete way. This is true even though the storyline is "opaque," as Ken Levine puts it.

Constants and Variables

But can *BioShock Infinite* really be considered a work of art? Is it similar to reading a novel in terms of your experience? If yes, we can call on concepts of aesthetics to help us understand what's going on when Booker and Elizabeth arrive in Rapture. Columbia is destroyed in 1912, while Rapture was only finished in 1951, and Booker and Elizabeth arrive there in 1960. This is not like the alternate realities of the Lutece "twins" where Booker does not give up his daughter or where Columbia survives and attacks New York City in 1983–84. The latter are variants of what happens in *BioShock Infinite*. We can think about them as "what could have been" or "what will be if this and that." But what the hell is Rapture doing there?

My answer relies on a term of literary criticism: "meta-fiction." "Meta" originates in Greek and means "after" or "beyond." In many contemporary uses, it has to do with "aboutness": meta-language is a language about language, meta-theory is a theory about theories, and so on. You can call the world of *BioShock Infinite* a "meta-universe," a universe of universes. The term meta-fiction, fiction about fiction, is mostly applied to modern and contemporary works of art—works of art that are "self-conscious" or "self-referential," works of art that call attention to being works of art. Novels often do this by telling stories about an author composing the story or about the reader reading it. Movies can be about people making a movie. (The hip reaction to this is: "Wow, that movie was so meta!")[7]

But what does this have to do with *BioShock Infinite*? As outrageous as it sounds, I think this is the only way to explain the appearance of Rapture in the game. In forums and comments, people have tried to set up explicit connections between the two cities, somehow forcing them into the same universe. Is Rapture the same as Columbia sunk under the sea? Is Comstock the same person as Andrew Ryan in a different alternate universe? Such understandings seem unwarranted. Playing through *BioShock Infinite*, there are no allusions at all to Rapture. In the scene when you travel to the future, to New Year's Eve of 1983, going into 1984 (a gentle nod to George Orwell), seeing Columbia attack New York City, you don't get any references to Rapture. The developers know better than anyone that their previous two games were set in a really cool underwater city called Rapture. If they wanted to make an explicit connection between the two storylines this way, they would have made it.

Consider what Grant Tavinor says about the original *BioShock*:

> The metaphor of being immersed in a fictional world is surely not accidental—*BioShock* is self-aware in a way that draws attention to its nature as a video game and as a fictional world into which players step as actors.[8]

This is crucial in why Booker and Elizabeth arrive in Rapture. The Rapture scene is the prelude to the sequence with infinite lighthouses. This is about telling stories. You see how the "meta" is creeping in: the makers of *BioShock Infinite* reflect on the potential of video games to tell stories. In a sense, *BioShock Infinite* is a video game about video games, particularly about video game stories and worlds. When Elizabeth says, "there's always a lighthouse, there's always a man, there's always a city," she doesn't just mean Booker's 123 attempts to defeat Comstock and rescue her. *BioShock* has been about creating awesome worlds that players can inhabit and explore, and in which they can follow intriguing storylines. These are constant features, just as the lighthouses, the main characters, and the cities are. They are always there. What is variable is whether you go up to the sky or under the sea.

A lighthouse, a man, a city. This is almost saying: we've created a fictional world (city) into which you, the player (man) can enter through a "doorway" (lighthouse). I'd conjecture that *BioShock Infinite* is called "*Infinite*" precisely because of the infinite lighthouses that appear to Booker and Elizabeth in the weird space they cross close to the ending. Infinite lighthouses mean infinite stories—stories that take place in Rapture, stories in Columbia, stories in other video games, in other worlds that are experienced a bit differently by each one of us playing them. *BioShock Infinite* is meta-fictional even in its title: it is about the possibility of infinite stories.

"Constants and variables"—Booker echoes Elizabeth's words, trying to comprehend them. These words are about Booker's previous 122 journeys to Columbia, which are forgotten, but they are also about the constants and variables of the alternate universes. Sometimes it seems like a constant that Booker was part of the Wounded Knee Massacre and it's a variable that he went through with the baptism afterwards and turned into Comstock. The ending of the game offers another possibility: a variable of Booker's being alive to become Comstock. Many possible Elizabeths appear and kill him at the baptism by drowning him, effectively destroying the possibility of Booker becoming Comstock. These are constants and variables of the alternate universes in *BioShock Infinite*. And then, sometimes Booker is a private investigator in Rapture, sometimes he is called Jack and Comstock is Andrew Ryan. These are constants and variables of the meta-universe that is *BioShock*.

Lighthouses, men, and cities. These are archetypes. The word comes from Greek: "*arkhe*" is something like a primitive or a foundation, put together with "*tupos*," which means model. An archetype is an original model on which later instantiations are created. *BioShock* makes lighthouses into archetypes with symbolic meaning. There are two lighthouses: one offers entry into Rapture, the other into Columbia. What is common to both of them is the symbolic property of offering entry into these fictional worlds. This is what "being a lighthouse" means in *BioShock*. It's like when you open a book or when the room in the cinema goes dark. "They are doors," says Elizabeth.

The notion of archetypes was used influentially by the psychoanalyst Carl Gustav Jung (1875–1961). Jung thought that the human psyche has ancient archetypes in what he termed the "collective unconscious."[9] What he meant by this is that these archetypes exist in your mind as well as my mind from birth in the same way, without you or me necessarily being aware of them. These archetypes can explain the common structural features of ancient myths and religions. For example, the recurring symbolic image of "the mother" is present in many cultures. Like most stories, the narratives of the *BioShock* series use archetypes. And again, this helps to make the case that *BioShock Infinite* is a work of art, similar to novels and movies. It's a work of art because it uses similar techniques, resources, and methods to tell its stories. Not only does *BioShock Infinite* use various archetypal images, it reflects on using them. It reflects on storytelling just as modern meta-fictional works of art do. The alternate universes and worlds of *BioShock Infinite* are not only about the machinations of the Lutece "twins." They are about the ways in which the *BioShock* series goes about telling its stories.

Archetypes found their way into the immensely popular theories of Joseph Campbell (1904–87). Campbell believed that stories around the world exhibit the same archetypal structure: the "monomyth" or the "hero's journey."[10] Basically, what you have in various tales from various cultures is the main character who departs (Departure) from the everyday world to go through the initiation (Initiation), to have adventures and to beat the challenges that lie ahead, and then to return (Return) home triumphantly. Narratives from ancient Greek myths to novels like *The Lord of the Rings* to movies like *Star Wars* and games like *Mass Effect* exhibit this common structure of the hero's journey. If you think about it, *BioShock Infinite* has this structure as well. At the beginning, all we know is that the (anti-)hero, Booker, comes from an ordinary gambling-debt background. He believes (falsely) that he has to rescue a girl from a city to "wipe away" his debt. On the boat, approaching the lighthouse, the Departure stage begins. Booker enters the lighthouse and the fantastic adventure starts through superpowers, tyrannical preachers, and motorized soldiers, signaling the Initiation stage. At the end, Booker returns to a very different reality than he left. So the structure is there, but it is twisted by multiple realities.

The Illusion of Choice

Noël Carroll, a prominent American philosopher of art, argues that art shouldn't be defined by essential qualities or conditions. Instead, if we can tell a coherent story about how a particular work descends from the tradition of other works, then we have a good chance of saying "yes, this is a work of art".[11] The genre of video games is still very young, compared to the thousands of years of drama, to the centuries of novels, and to moviemaking that began at the end of the nineteenth century. So it has to walk before it can fly. But to me, it has a damn good chance of flying. The scene with Rapture and then the overwhelming ocean of infinite lighthouses are there to show you that video games can tell great stories, and that by telling great stories they participate in the same tradition as other artistic media. Now, I don't want to say that I'd rate *BioShock Infinite* as highly as the great novels of the past centuries. What I want to say is that the comparison is not as unimaginable as some people thinking of the arts would have it.

Some players have criticized *BioShock Infinite* for its lack of inter-activity. There's no choice between "being good" and "being evil" that would lead to different endings. The original *BioShock* had three endings depending on your actions concerning the Little Sisters. In *BioShock Infinite*, there's no such interactivity between player actions and story conclusions. Some would say that this makes *BioShock Infinite* into more of a movie than an actual video game. If *BioShock Infinite* can be claimed to be an independent work of art, it needs to be a work of art distinct from movies, even if it shares qualities with them. It needs to make use of the possibilities that are inherent in the medium of interactive video games.

The main problem here is that it's really hard to tell a good story when the audience can influence the story. This is the reason video games sometimes take the control out of the hands of their players in the form of, for example, cutscenes. If you had freedom to interact when Booker is killed by the many alternate versions of Elizabeth in the end, you might run away or kill an Elizabeth or two. It would've been funny, but it would also have significantly reduced the intellectual and emotional impact that *BioShock Infinite* has, and would totally have gone against a coherent ending to the story. There are events that simply must happen for the game to be able to tell its story. This is the same even with sandbox games like the *Grand Theft Auto* series or *Skyrim*. Even though you have much more freedom to do as you please in those games, to follow the main quest or main storyline, things simply must happen. *BioShock Infinite* reflects on this on a very deep level. It has integrated into its story the whole quantum physics–Schrödinger's cat–multiverse business. The infinite possibilities are drowned in one linear playthrough.

And yet, you can choose the bird or the cage. Ultimately, it doesn't matter what you choose. You are like Booker being totally oblivious about his previous journeys to Columbia. You have the illusion of choice; the outcomes will be the same. The way in which *BioShock Infinite* explains this is that every choice is made in a parallel universe. If you choose the bird in one universe, you choose the cage in another. It doesn't influence the ending or the gameplay, and yes, it can seem that *BioShock Infinite* pulls the player along a fixed rail where the only "meaningful" choice is whether to blast out a Murder of Crows or a Shock Jockey Vigor. *BioShock Infinite* seems to be a work of art when it tells its story, but it doesn't seem to be one when it comes to its gameplay. This has a lot to do with the lack of interactivity. However, *BioShock Infinite* is still one of the greatest video game stories and worlds of all time. In this, it represents a big step towards artful video game design, and in the future, if Ken Levine is able to pull off his "narrative legos" idea or something similar, it might just be the game with an artistically captivating story, combined with innovative and interactive gameplay, that offers a uniquely aesthetic experience distinct from movies. In the meantime, *BioShock* succeeds in showing that the possibilities for artful storytelling are infinite.

Notes

1. Brian Crecente, "Ken Levine on His Secret Post-BioShock 'Thought Experiment,'" last modified October 9, 2013, http://www.polygon.com/2013/10/9/4816828/ken-levines-next-big-thing-isnt-so-much-a-game-as-it-is-a-reinvention.
2. Jonathan Gottschall, *The Storytelling Animal* (Boston, MA: Houghton Mifflin Harcourt, 2012).
3. Check out this article where game designers talk about the future of video game storytelling: Lucy O'Brian, "The Future of Video Game Storytelling," last modified January 12, 2014, http://www.ign.com/articles/2014/01/13/the-future-of-video-game-storytelling.

4. This is not to say that gameplay and story are disconnected. Some players might go on discovering the world in order to be able to make better decisions. What is surprising about *Infinite* is that decisions do not influence the outcome of the story.

5. John Dewey, *Art as Experience* (New York: Perigee Books, 1980; original work published, 1934).

6. "A work of art elicits and accentuates this quality of being a whole and of belonging to the larger, all-inclusive, whole which is the universe in which we live. This fact, I think, is the explanation of that feeling of exquisite intelligibility and clarity we have in the presence of an object that is experienced with aesthetic intensity... We are, as it were, introduced into a world beyond this world which is nevertheless the deeper reality of the world in which we live in our ordinary experiences... We are carried to a refreshed attitude toward the circumstances and exigencies of ordinary experience... Just because it is a full and intense experience, [art] keeps alive the power to experience the common world in its fullness." Dewey, *Art as Experience*, as quoted in Richard Eldridge, "Dewey's Aesthetics," in *The Cambridge Companion to Dewey*, ed. Molly Cochran (Cambridge: Cambridge University Press, 2010), 248.

7. Sometimes characters in these products can realize that they are fictional characters. See the movie called *Stranger Than Fiction* or the play *The Stanley Parable*, where the narrator is aware of being a narrator who tells the story and doesn't hesitate to share his awareness of it.

8. Grant Tavinor, *The Art of Videogames* (Malden, MA: Wiley-Blackwell, 2009), 61.

9. Carl Gustav Jung, *The Archetypes and the Collective Unconscious,* 2nd edn, trans. R. F. C. Hull (Princeton, NJ: Princeton University Press, 1981).

10. Joseph Campbell, *The Hero with a Thousand Faces* (New York: Pantheon Books, 1949).

11. Noël Carroll, *Philosophy of Art* (London: Routledge, 1999).

14

Have You Ever Been to Rapture?

BioShock as an Introduction to Phenomenology

Stefan Schevelier

I'm standing in a poorly lit room. Across the room stands a large desk, covered with notes. A corkboard fills the wall, also covered with notes. Bloody letters run across the center. "Would you kindly" they read...

I am about to enter Andrew Ryan's office, the office of a man who controls an entire city on the bottom of the ocean. After my plane crashed I found a hidden society where market capitalism reigns supreme, where I've used technology to alter my own genetic code, and where I've battled the city's deranged citizens. I am about to step into the office of the man who has tried to kill me from the moment I arrived and who, as I've just discovered, is my father.

"In the end, what separates a man from a slave?" he asks me as I enter. "A man chooses... A slave obeys!" he answers. I am here because I want to kill this man, but my controller does not respond and my sense of immersion is gone. The illusion of freedom shatters, I have no choice in this matter. I am but a slave. "A man chooses... A slave obeys!" he repeats, and—proving that he's a man and I'm but a slave—he orders me to kill him. Again my controller does not respond as I beat his head in. Andrew Ryan chooses his own death and is therefore a man, while I remain but a slave.

There is something very unsettling about this scene the first time you play it. In part, this has to do with the fact that you watch yourself bash Andrew Ryan's head in with a golf club, but there's more to it than that. It is also unsettling because it allows you to experience

BioShock and Philosophy: Irrational Game, Rational Book, First Edition. Edited by Luke Cuddy.
© 2015 John Wiley & Sons, Inc. Published 2015 by John Wiley & Sons, Inc.

what it is like to lose your sense of freedom. Up until that point in the story, the player feels as if the story is his or her own. Note how often I used the word "I" to make the story mine. It would be pointless to refer to the protagonist with his name "Jack," as if I could be separated from the protagonist of *BioShock*'s tale. There is no such difference when I'm completely immersed in Rapture. For all intents and purposes, *BioShock* feels as if it is my own story, it feels as if I experience the story of this man who travels to the bottom of the ocean. In every sense of the word, it feels as if I really am in Rapture. This explains why it is all the more shocking when the controller suddenly does not respond. My sense of immersion is shattered and I find myself playing a game, on a couch, behind a screen. When I no longer control the actions on screen, the game's story is no longer mine, but returns to being Jack's story. This rupture reveals a fundamental aspect of our experience; namely, that my actions have a sense of *mineness*.

Our experience of daily life is filled with—or really is only possible through—characteristics such as *mineness*. Phenomenology is a school of philosophy that is interested in these peculiar characteristics of experience. For example, it is interested in how experience always has a time and a place, how it is always experienced by a body, and how it is always an experience *of* something. In short, phenomenology is the study of the world as it appears to us.

Prometheus Falls

I'll assume that you've played *BioShock* or *BioShock Infinite* at least once. Now, suppose you want to tell someone what it was like to play those games—not just that you had a good time playing them, but really tell them *what it is like*. Imagine, if you will, that you are to review the game for a website or magazine.

You could start with the game's technical details, since every game is made using specific software, requires certain hardware to run, uses textures of a certain resolution, has character models with a specific polygon count, and so on. These technical details are interesting, but mostly relevant for the visual aspect of the video game and they don't tell you much about *what it is like* to play the game.

You could also enlist the help of science. For example, you could stick someone in a brain scanner and let him or her play the game, while you measure brain activity. Although that would certainly be interesting, it still wouldn't tell you much about that person's actual experience. In a famous paper, contemporary philosopher Thomas Nagel argued that science is rather useless when it comes to describing experiences.[1] He used the following example to explain why. Suppose you know everything there is to know about a bat's use of echolocation: you've read every book on the subject and have studied bats extensively. Would that give you any idea of what it is like for the bat actually to use echolocation? No, it wouldn't. It would be like trying to describe color to a blind person. Similarly, if you knew everything there is to know about a person's state while playing *BioShock*—if you could describe the exact neurons firing, the synapses responding, and so on—you still wouldn't know *what it is like* to play *BioShock*, and that's precisely what phenomenology is interested in.

What does phenomenology have to offer that science cannot? Phenomenology is well suited to dealing with problems that are subjective, have to do with our experience of the world around us, with our experience of ourselves, and with things that are only available to us through introspection. So, science might explain how to build a city on the ocean floor, but it would have a difficult time explaining what it feels like to lose your sense of *mineness* when you play *BioShock*.

Plasmids, Vigors, and Other Methods

A scientist hides in his laboratory, a poet retreats into the woods, and a writer resorts to cigarettes and alcohol. What is the phenomenologist's method? Some philosophers would argue that there are a great number of phenomenological methods, but I think they basically fall into two categories:

- *The phenomenological tradition.* First, there's the difficult method of conducting an actual phenomenological investigation. Edmund

Husserl (1859–1938)—a.k.a. the godfather of phenomenology—originally developed phenomenology as a means of grounding mathematics and the natural sciences. By concentrating on your experience of reality, by forgetting everything you were ever told about the world, and by thinking really hard about the essence of your experience, you can produce something that science and mathematics can't: an idea about the structure of your everyday experience. Luckily for us, philosophers like Martin Heidegger (1889–1976), Jean-Paul Sartre (1905–80), and Maurice Merleau-Ponty (1908–61), to name just a few, have all come to phenomenological insights that can be applied directly to your experience of *BioShock*. Their work constitutes a proverbial walkthrough or cheat-code of phenomenology, a veritable library of phenomenological analyses.

- *Art as phenomenology.* Secondly, art also functions as a phenomenological method. This method is most important to our discussion of *BioShock*, and Merleau-Ponty's consideration of the phenomenological function of art is the best example. His work is mainly concerned with painting, but it can usefully be extended to movies and video games.[2]

Let's start with Merleau-Ponty's description of the art of painting. He gives two accounts of what a painter does when he paints, for example, a young woman like Elizabeth.[3] On the first account, called naturalism, the artist understands the object of his painting, in this case Elizabeth. He must comprehend the way her muscles move beneath her skin, the properties and texture of her dress, and the characteristics of the light falling on her skin through the open window. This knowledge serves to produce the most precise representation of the painted object. On the second account, the phenomenological one, the artist aims to do something else entirely. Instead of focusing on the object of his painting, he pays attention to his own subjective experience. He notices how his eyes are focused on Elizabeth's eyes, on the faint light that catches some of her hair, and he notices how he gets nervous as she moves around, unable to sit still for the duration of the session. His aim isn't to represent her eyes very accurately, to catch precisely the right tone of the light, or her movements. Instead, the artist aims to capture his experience of the scene in his painting and, through the painting, tries to reproduce his focus and anxiety in whoever looks at the painting.

Just as Merleau-Ponty distinguishes two types of painters, we can distinguish two types of film directors. Analogous to naturalism in painting, a filmmaker can aim simply to capture a scene objectively. Just as the painter has his paintbrush, the director has a camera that allows her to capture an image of a particular object. What is more, the camera allows the director to encapsulate movement, change, and transformation. This allows her to portray a whole new dimension of her subjective experience. Whereas the painter has only one painting to capture his experience, the film director has 24 frames per second to do so. Not only is she now able to illustrate the way she focuses on Elizabeth's eyes, the camera also allows her to demonstrate how her own eyes wander over time.

Now, let's move on to games. Games add yet another dimension to the moving images of film: interaction. In *Infinite*, players have the ability to walk through a scene and interact with Elizabeth. This allows the game director to re-create the very familiar experience of interaction in a work of art. This enlarges the artist's potential to capture and produce subjective experiences, but also requires a terribly complex game world. Surfaces must reflect light, objects must offer resistance, movement must produce sound, bricks must fall, birds must fly, and so on. It also requires a terribly complex Elizabeth. This game world, Elizabeth included, is a work of art in its own right, and Ken Levine and his team are its artists.

In order to create these worlds, they must have had certain scientific ideas about the reflective capacity of surfaces, the resistance of objects, and sound production. More importantly, though, they must have also had some, conscious or subconscious, phenomenological ideas about *what it is like* to be around a girl like Elizabeth. Only the synthesis of those two sets of ideas could have produced a work of art such as *Infinite*. The ideas that ground our experience of our time with Elizabeth are phenomenological in the sense that they are essentially ideas about the structure of our conscious experience. *Infinite* is defined by the artists' and programmers' ability to convey those ideas. So, *Infinite* is phenomenologically interesting because the game's designers have poured phenomenological ideas into Columbia and Elizabeth, which we can then read as if they were books containing a phenomenological analysis of reality. Chris Kline, *BioShock*'s lead programmer, confirms this in the game's "making of," when he mentions the question that drove the game's design process. The team continually asked themselves: "What is this experience we are trying to make?"[4] This question is a testament to the phenomenological attitude of the game's production team and is what makes them artistic phenomenologists.

Now Would You Kindly Pick Up That Controller?

"Cut to the chase," you might say. "How do I conduct such a phenomenological investigation?" Should I be playing the game while I analyze it phenomenologically? What should I look for while I play the game? What type of questions should I ask myself when I analyze *BioShock*? When will I know that I'm done?

On the one hand, following Heidegger, we can assume that if you've played a good immersive game like *BioShock* once, you're set for your analysis. Replaying the game is only necessary if you played the game superficially, or played it long ago. The *mineness* that the game evokes is enough to make the game feel a part of your life. Reflecting on your memories of *BioShock* should be enough to bring you to some phenomenological insights.

On the other hand, following Merleau-Ponty's artistic method, one can argue that replaying the game is not such a bad idea. You should want to play the game as if you haven't played it before, naively. Let yourself be immersed in the game's story. You should look for moments when the "suspension of disbelief" breaks, when you're aware that you're playing a video game instead of living it.[5] Ask yourself: What makes this experience so believable? Why does this strange world suck me in like it's the real world? What are the things that break the immersion and certainly aren't part of my everyday experience?

There's a section in *Infinite* that I think explains very well what kind of questions you should be asking. It's when you help Elizabeth escape Monument Island and she asks you: "What am I?" Having just found out that she's been held captive like a lab rat for years, she wonders what makes her special. Having spent her whole life in isolation on Monument Island, she's read every book she could get her hands on, but she doesn't know much about herself. Why can she open portals to other dimensions? Where does she come from? What makes her special? In short: What is she?

You actually spend a good amount of time finding an answer to her questions. It's one of the things that drive the main storyline. You listen to Voxophones, talk to Elizabeth, study her behavior, and so on. About halfway through *Infinite* you even forget about bringing Elizabeth back to New York and fully commit yourself to her quest, helping her find the answers she's looking for.

This changes radically in the game's final hours, when Elizabeth regains full control over her tearing powers, and shows you a multitude of lighthouses, which represent alternate universes. As you walk from lighthouse to lighthouse, Elizabeth talks about the constants and variables across universes. She explains how behind each door lies a universe that contains a man, a woman, a city, and a lighthouse. Somehow, Booker is one of the multiverse's constants. This raises the question: "What is Booker?" or better yet: "What is the player?" What makes you, the player, a constant across Booker's, and your own, dimension? *Infinite*'s real question is: "What am I, that I can experience all these worlds?"

Time to Put Some Sweat on That Brow

Everything is set for our actual investigation. At this point you might choose either to (re)play the *BioShock* games and (re)gain some familiarity with them, or read on, and see what I think is phenomenologically interesting about *BioShock*.

Let's start with how we killed Andrew Ryan in the first *BioShock* game. I've briefly sketched what happens when you kill your father in the introduction to this chapter, in an attempt to explain what phenomenology is, but the scene is also a playful meditation on *what it is like* to be free.

The first important part of the passage is: "I am standing in a poorly lit room." It explains where I am at the moment; a picture of a room should appear in your mind's eye. "I have used technology to alter my own genetic code and I have battled the city's deranged citizens." This describes my history and paints the context of the actions. I am heading toward "the office of the man who has tried to kill me from the moment I arrived and, as I've just discovered, is my father." I have come here to kill this man, Andrew Ryan. Ken Levine and his team have built a game—or maybe we should say that they've created a world—that draws me in and gives purpose to the choices I make. Nobody has forced me to play the game up to this point: I've moved freely through Rapture, chosen a specific set of Plasmids and tonics, and have spared or smothered Little Sisters. Those choices made sense at the time: I went in that direction to gather a key, that Plasmid helped me overcome a certain foe, and I've killed that Little Sister because...

Or so I thought. "The illusion of freedom shatters" as I enter the room. I can no longer control my actions on the screen. The bond between the protagonist and me is broken. Andrew Ryan explains why: I am but a slave, genetically altered to follow the commands of Atlas—a.k.a. Frank Fontaine—Ryan's great rival. What seemed like acts of my own free will were actually orders of powers beyond my control. That little phrase "Would you kindly..." was not a sign of courtesy, but in fact a genetically encoded phrase that triggered me to follow Atlas's commands. Ryan, in a twisted act of self-assertion, uses the phrase to order me to kill him, thereby proving that he is free and I am in chains. For the first time, my actions do not make any sense. I do not want to kill Andrew Ryan now that I know that I'm nothing more than a tool. Or perhaps I do want to kill him, but not this way. Anyway, the actions on screen are no longer my actions.

Now that I am thrown out of Rapture, and realize that I'm simply a man playing a game, the distinction between protagonist and player becomes clear again. I can now see that I am betrayed on the level of both the player and the protagonist. Both as player and as protagonist, I've done what I've done under false pretenses. Jack, the protagonist, confronted Ryan, believing that Atlas would provide him with a way out of Rapture on his defeat. We, as gamers, assumed, as Jack himself did, that we were real human beings with a history and a family, that our choices were in accordance with who Jack was. Ryan's words reveal that our choices were not in accordance with the world we've constructed. As Robert Lutece writes in *Barriers to Trans-Dimensional Travel*: "The mind of the subject will desperately struggle to create memories where none exist..."[6] Even more so than Booker and Elizabeth in *Infinite*, we, the players, are the ones doing the transdimensional traveling. On top of Levine's Rapture, we create our own Rapture that gives meaning to the things we do. We constantly try to create a narrative, complete with past and future, that explains our actions. It is phenomenologically interesting that freedom requires such a narrative, and that it requires so little of it.

Welcome to Rapture

This takes us to the second phenomenological theme: the worlds that *BioShock* and *Infinite* present. When I look at games phenomenologically, I try to take them seriously. This is not difficult. A good game makes it easy for the player to identify with its protagonist. The player determines the character's movement and actions. When the protagonist is addressed, by other characters for example, the player feels that he or she is addressed. The distinction, then, between the player and the protagonist fades and the player *is* the protagonist.

Once you are comfortable in the role of protagonist, you are easily absorbed by the worlds of Rapture and Columbia. They present you with an underwater, capitalist utopia and a city in the clouds. "What if...," *BioShock* asks, "the world is not ruled by petty morality, but by the invisible hand of the marketplace," a world that the player soon finds to be a dystopia rather than a utopia. "What if...," *Infinite* asks, "a racist prophet builds a city in the clouds." In interviews and talks, Ken Levine hints at the design philosophy behind this world: immersion.[7]

Heidegger famously argued that a hammer shows itself best in one of two moments, when it is used or when it breaks. We could ask the same thing about the *BioShock* games. What makes and breaks our sense of immersion in these games?

What had me immersed the most while playing the *BioShock* games were the parts when you simply scour Rapture and Columbia for goods and bits of storytelling. These are the moments when the lines between player and protagonist blur most. Take one of the first scenes of *BioShock*, when you visit a trashed New Year's Eve party at Kashmir's restaurant. You stumble on a couple of Splicers, take them out, and start looking for supplies before you find an audio diary by Diane McClintock. While you wade through the water, empty bottles, and the ruins of the restaurant, you hear Diane murmuring about being lonely, before being attacked by other Splicers. It's the little details in this place that really suck you in: the pay phones by the entrance, the argument between the Splicer couple on the lower floor, the sign by the entrance saying "Happy New Year 1959," or the party hat by Diane's audio diary.

Infinite has similarly immersive scenes: the game's lighthouse intro is a fine example, as is the final hour of the game. When we think about what makes these scenes immersive, there are a couple of things that come to mind. First, they present the player with a coherent world. The restaurant's got a closed-off kitchen, a men's and a ladies' room, enough seats to accommodate a sizable New Year's Eve party, enough booze to last till morning, and so on. You'll never stop to question whether this is a credible restaurant. Objectives also create a sense of immersion. In some of the most immersive scenes the player's got a sense of urgency. For example, "I must find supplies," "I must get out of this tower, it's falling apart," or simply, "What the hell is going on?" We can only focus on so many things, and if something urgent requires our attention we can't stop to question the credibility of Rapture.

At other times *BioShock* fails to suspend your disbelief, reminding you that Rapture isn't real or that Columbia is a fiction. First off, a bug in the game is guaranteed to make you lose your sense of immersion: it might be a character stuck in a corner, a disappearing item, or a texture that doesn't load properly (or maybe you've just got a shitty computer). Drugs and mental disorders aside, the world around us isn't buggy. Secondly, appreciating a work of art requires a certain setting. The first and second *BioShock* games in particular, rocking more of a horror vibe than *Infinite*, are best played in a dark environment on a decent display, with a nice set of speakers so you can hear that Splicer behind you. Playing the game on an old TV or PC, in broad daylight, in a noisy room, brings in outside interference and wrecks our sense of immersion. Thirdly, some details are very important. For instance, Jack is always silent, while Booker tends to shout quite a bit. Not having a voice is a particularly immersive quality, because everything your character says is an opportunity to wonder "Would I have said that?" or "That's not what my voice sounds like," and so on.

Is a Man Not Entitled to the Sweat of His Brow?

The phenomenological relevance of these insights is that they reveal something about ourselves. Through these exercises we come to know about the constants and variables of our existence. This short intro-duction should enable you to perform your very own phenomenolo-gical investigation. If you haven't already done so, you might want to replay the first *BioShock* or revisit *Infinite*. See if you can uncover what makes these games reflective of our everyday experience. Try to uncover what the constants and variables are between our world and that of video games. When you feel that you've got a good grasp on the phenomenology of *BioShock*, you can try to extend your analysis to other games, and other works of art. Or, if you feel really comfortable, you can delve into your everyday experience.

Notes

1. Thomas Nagel, "What Is It Like to Be a Bat?" *Philosophical Review* 83 (1974): 435–450.
2. John B. Brough, "Showing and Seeing—Film as Phenomenology," in *Art and Phenomenology*, ed. Joseph D. Parry (London: Routledge, 2011), 193.
3. Maurice Merleau-Ponty, *The World of Perception* (London: Routledge, 2004), 52–54.
4. 2K Games. *Welcome to Rapture—The Making of BioShock*. 2007.
5. Ibid.
6. This quotation is the very opening scene to *BioShock Infinite*. The game starts with a passage from a fictional book by one of *Infinite*'s characters, Robert Lutece, which is the motto to *BioShock Infinite*.
7. Two examples are the above-mentioned *Welcome to Rapture—The Making of BioShock* and Irrational Games, "Ken Levine Filmed at a BAFTA Q&A," *YouTube* video, 1:44:55, March 16, 2013, http://www.youtube.com/watch?v=Efv9Mgwk8SU.

15

"Evolve today!"
Human Enhancement Technologies in the *BioShock* Universe

Simon Ledder

> Imagine if you could be smarter, stronger, healthier. What if you could even have amazing powers, light fires with your mind … That's what Plasmids do for a man.

Contrary to the optimism of Atlas's words above, my first discovery of Plasmids in *BioShock* was quite unpleasant. I walked up to a vending machine and, before I knew it, flashes of lightning flew between my arms. I lost control of motor function and fell over a railing into unconsciousness. After this first shocking interaction, my use of Plasmids and gene tonics became an intuitive way of dealing with my surroundings, and especially my enemies.

My first encounter with Plasmids in the world outside *BioShock* was not nearly as eventful. In the contemporary field of bioethics, there is a discussion about Plasmids. Well, not exactly, but about something similar: the so-called human enhancement technologies, for both physical and cognitive improvements. Naturally, this raises questions: Should we prohibit such enhancement technologies? Or are we morally obliged to use them? Are they problematic in themselves; and what would be the consequences of using them?

In the bioethics literature, there is a distinction between therapeutic practices and enhancement technologies. Some types of medicine, such as pharmaceuticals, or some invasive procedures into the brain that allow individuals to "restore" themselves to

BioShock and Philosophy: Irrational Game, Rational Book, First Edition. Edited by Luke Cuddy.
© 2015 John Wiley & Sons, Inc. Published 2015 by John Wiley & Sons, Inc.

"normal" abilities, seem to be met with universal approval. But what do we think about "healthy" individuals who want to "enhance" their own biology?

The Plasmids in *BioShock* are essentially enhancement technologies for "healthy" individuals. You can actively use your EVE to fire electric bolts from your hand, or manipulate the minds and bodies of others, or trick the sensors of bots and cameras. To access these abilities, the human body in *BioShock* has to be altered with ADAM, stem cells harvested from sea slugs and then genetically manipulated to produce cells that the human body does not have naturally. The process results in enhanced humans like the Little Sisters and the Big Daddies.

What Exactly Are They Researching?

Although the sea slug in *BioShock* is a work of fiction, in the real world researchers are investigating species-transcending gene technology. In fact, synthetic biology is based on the idea of sewing genes together artificially. The results of this research might someday be applied to make enhanced humans like the Big Daddies.

Of course, *BioShock* takes place in a cruel world. No researcher in our world is allowed to experiment on human subjects without their informed consent. That means no Little Sisters or Big Daddies in the immediate future. Real-world scientists have to deal with what they've got. For example, scientists have developed forms of gene therapy, such as somatic cell therapy, that allow them to prevent future illnesses, disorders, or abnormalities. Or on a more radical level, your germ line can be altered. This means that some DNA in your cells is changed or eliminated so that the problematic sequence of genetic material will not be passed on to your children or any future generations.

Also of interest is pre-implantation genetic diagnosis, a process in which embryos are produced in an environment that is not a womb (in vitro). The embryos are then presented for the parents to select. Only the selected embryo survives and is transplanted. The selection process means that parents have the opportunity to design a child. They can decide the sex of the child, remove undesirable genetic traits, and choose which parent the child will resemble. But is it moral to manipulate a child in its biological core? And if so, what criteria should guide the design?

In Rapture, Dr. Suchong developed methods of mental conditioning and growth acceleration. Likewise, Dr. Tenenbaum designed a genetic process to turn small girls into ADAM-harvesting Little Sisters. *BioShock* science also produces the Big Daddies, equipped with strength above human average; their bodies and their diving suits are grafted together.

BioShock makes apparent the usefulness of biological enhancements, but also warns us about the potential dangers of playing with biology. If future developments in the real world made it possible to have a third arm, or extra-sensory perception, would you be tempted? Some researchers—and artists like Stelarc and Orlan—actually try to find out if that's possible and what that means.

Wait, You Want to Change the Nature of Humanity?

Not everyone is in favor of human enhancement technologies. Their opponents fear that some procedures might change what it means to be human on a fundamental level. But what is human nature? For some thinkers, human nature is best represented in the idea of a "species-typical normal functional organization."[1] This means that humans have some specific needs (like food, sleep, communication) and the necessary abilities to fulfill these needs (like two arms, two legs, and a clearly defined organism). What if our human dignity depends on these endowments? What if human nature has an essential core that is not changeable without threatening our sense of morality and the social order?[2]

Some opponents of human enhancement even go a few steps further. They ask what will happen to non-enhanced mortals if we create enhanced superhumans. What if the latter have the power to subdue us?[3] The advent of Splicers in Rapture might give a preview of what it would be like to be overwhelmed by uncontrollable, enhanced individuals that don't have any connection to humanity.

There is also the question of authenticity. Does a human lose a part of herself when she merges her body with technology? If our body has been formed by nature, how can we dare to change that?

But Isn't Human Enhancement a Big Leap Forward?

On the other side, some philosophers enthusiastically favor enhancement technologies. A few consider themselves "transhumanists," which means they want to develop a kind of human that goes beyond our current understanding of human nature. Like their opponents, these proponents of biotechnology also argue that humans have limits; however, they claim that humans can and should overcome these limits with the help of technology. The promises of enhancement are great: not only could combat and hacking skills be increased—which we can experience when playing *BioShock*—but our daily lives could be much easier. Why carry heavy bags if it's possible just to float them through the air with telekinesis? No philosopher, of course, mentions this particular possibility, because telekinesis is too far out of reach to happen any time soon. Yet, there are some ideas—like uploading a person's consciousness to a gigantic electronic network and being rid of the physical body—that transhumanists actually do consider.[4] This sounds a bit like the mind and memory storage that Eleanor Lamb does while collecting ADAM in *BioShock 2*.

You don't have to be a transhumanist to favor enhancement technologies, though. What if you could be more productive by thinking faster or working longer hours? The promise of increased productivity through faster neural transmission and sustained concentration has highlighted the field of neuropharmacology. Pills have been developed to increase productivity. Although the side effects are still unclear, such drugs already are in use.[5]

In *BioShock* you won't find Plasmids that increase your cognitive or emotional capabilities. *BioShock* is a digital game, and the types of Plasmids you are given are adequate to the challenges you encounter. But the game's focus isn't so far from reality. Much of the scientific research into enhancement technologies is done by the military, the purpose, of course, being to better equip soldiers for combat.

Don't Tell Me What to Do with My Body!

Contemporary philosopher Alan Sandberg argues in favor of the individual's right to change the body.[6] According to Sandberg, a government has no right to tell you what to do with your hair, clothes, or body as long as no harm befalls others (harming yourself is another topic). If you have ownership over your body, why shouldn't you have the right to use enhancement technologies?

This would have to work on a voluntary, individual level. In Rapture, Andrew Ryan decided not to impose regulations on ADAM because he was certain the market would regulate any problems. Of course, we need to beware when the government gets in the business of human enhancement. Just think of the eugenics that started in the nineteenth century and culminated in the German National Socialist eugenics program in which 100,000 "disabled" persons were killed and 400,000 were sterilized.

The "morphological freedom"[7] to alter yourself is already here in a sense. Technology is increasingly pervasive and invasive, altering the way we perceive and interact with the world. Some philosophers insist that humans have always altered themselves because it's in humanity's nature to improve itself. Wouldn't it only be the logical, or even natural, next step to use technology to enhance our bodies?[8]

Some people might argue that our bodies are already altered anyway. In contrast to earlier times of human history, vaccinations are given as a standard preventive treatment to nearly everyone in the developed world. Some people use coffee and cigarettes all the time to manage their day—and according to *BioShock*, coffee and cigarettes increase your EVE. So what is the difference between coffee and cigarettes and other neuropharmacological enhancers? Is it that they are synthetically produced? Why should that be a problem? We live in the twenty-first century, after all. Instead of holding on to old-fashioned notions, perhaps we should use the scientific discoveries in any way that seems progressive for humanity. What if these enhancements, for example, would allow people to experience Mozart in a way never before possible?[9] We can hear these dreams in Suchong's praise of his work as well: "ADAM is a canvas of genetic modification. But Plasmids are the paint."

Who Profits from This?

One important criticism of human enhancement involves the question of social justice. Who could afford enhancements? What if only rich people could afford such technologies? The inequality of the haves and the have-nots would rise to a new level.[10] Can we allow these technologies if we strive for a just society?[11] But perhaps this would be only a temporary problem. At first the early adopters would have advantages, but eventually prices would decrease and everyone would have access to these technologies.[12]

Perhaps enhancement technologies would actually lead to greater social justice and equality by benefiting those who aren't as genetically gifted as others. As things stand, we are subject to the genetic lottery, but enhancement technologies would shift our fate "from chance to choice"[13] and level the playing field.

Then again, enhancement technologies may produce unwanted pressure, as when athletes feel they need to use steroids to keep pace with the competition. Likewise, if some people start to enhance themselves, others may feel pressured to do so as well.[14] In Rapture, we see the results of this spiral in the arms race during the Civil War. Combat Plasmids were in highest demand, which is hardly surprising because competition is vital to survival in such situations. Those who did not enhance were easily disposed of by the Splicers.

As a player, I experienced this upward spiral for myself during the game. The Electric Bolt Plasmid, which killed many enemies in the first few levels, was ineffective in the latter parts of the game. Suddenly the Splicers became immune to my hits of high voltage, and this required me to enhance myself further with the Electric Bolt 2. Doesn't this suggest that the use of enhancement technologies leads to a continual process of more and more invasive operations on ourselves to compete with other individuals—resulting, possibly, in addictions like the Splicers developed?

As some enhancement enthusiasts would say, this slippery slope is only dangerous if these technologies are unregulated. There should be regulations to ensure there is equal access to enhancements, and the use of enhancement technologies should not be made a prerequisite for any job that can be done without them. Wouldn't that ensure that no one has to use such technologies if they don't want to?[15]

Of course, maybe the whole idea of human enhancement technologies is just the latest manifestation of capitalism. In contemporary Western societies, people have to sell their powers of body and mind to earn money for food and shelter. They have to work constantly on their capacities, while also being flexible, to get a job in the current economy. In Andrew Ryan's view, any other form of society would be "parasitic."

In our world, we all have to optimize ourselves to compete against others, sometimes by any means necessary. So wouldn't it be a mistake to discuss enhancement technologies simply as an ethical issue, or even an issue of individual choice, without taking into account the socio-political context in which these technologies will be developed?[16]

In the real world there is also some concern about how research has merged in universities and in the pharmaceutical industry. Who regulates what research funding goes into the development of these technologies? And wouldn't it be more useful to do research on some conventionally therapeutic issues, like curing cancer, instead of delving into luxury products that only a few people can afford?[17]

We Would Program Our Children

During my voyage through Rapture in *BioShock*, I learned that I am a son of Andrew Ryan. Despite its advantages, such as the Vita-Chambers, my heritage also had some negative consequences. For example, Fontaine used all the possible technology to make me a tool for his purposes. My body and my mind were conditioned to respond automatically to phrases like "Would you kindly …" or "Code Yellow."

Since my birth in Rapture I was equipped to execute one task: to work against my father, Andrew Ryan, if Fontaine needed me to. This idea of "designing" people for specific purposes can also be found in pre-implantation genetic diagnosis. As the contemporary philosopher Jürgen Habermas argues, if parents choose their offspring's genes—like the sex, or a disposition to superior musical or physical abilities—do they not at the same time determine their child's future?[18] Wouldn't this poor child always know that he only exists because of his parents' preference for some genes? And if that's the only reason for his existence, could this child see himself as anything other than his parents' projection?

Of course, environment also has a major influence on a child's development. Only due to interaction with other humans will a child develop into an autonomous subject with free will; and isn't that the primary characteristic by which we define humanity? For Habermas, the human has its place somewhere above the biological. Culture is the precondition that allows us to talk on an equal level in rational discourse, and, again according to Habermas, the rational discourse between equal autonomous subjects is necessary for our society to thrive. If an individual had her genetic heritage manipulated, how could she still be such an autonomous subject? Could such an individual be held responsible for her actions?

Consider the connection to *BioShock*. As a player, I am shocked when suddenly, after hours of playing in the first-person perspective, I am stripped of all powers to act and just have to watch myself following the orders Andrew Ryan gave me to kill him. I am not able to express my free will, I am not the master of my actions. I act because I have to. We can read this experience of powerlessness as a metaphorical presentation of Habermas's argument.

But at Least the People with "Disabilities" Could Live a "Normal" Life

In *BioShock*, we find a typical argument concerning disability. An audio diary from Tenenbaum mentions a worker whose "hands were crippled" and who "could move his fingers for the first time after years" because he was bitten by a sea slug. Tenenbaum conducts her first experiments using this sea slug, eventually leading to the commercial production of ADAM.

Enhancement technologies are often described as beneficial for people who are disabled by our current standards, because with their bodies "improved" to the "normal" functioning, they will not "suffer" more in this world than anybody else will.[19] Some people argue that defining enhancement as "better than average" doesn't work. If those who are conventionally disabled use technology to get their bodies on to a "normal" level, this could already count as an enhancement.[20]

Generally speaking, the debate about enhancement technologies perpetuates the idea that a "disability" is a characteristic of an individual, and independent of any social or cultural factors that labeled something a disability in the first place. Different voices in the heterogeneous Disability Movement have criticized this individual perspective on disability for some time now. If our society's rules suppose that everyone has to be treated equally, how can it be necessary to change one's body and/or mind to fully participate?[21]

Some philosophers equate disability with "suffering," but this doesn't seem right.[22] As many disabled people have argued, their life can be as rewarding and joyful as any other person's, but they have to fight against many structural barriers. These barriers privilege people whose bodies fit normative ideals of ability. But a norm-adequate body is not required to live a happy life. There are many other factors that contribute to happiness and quality of life, which are overlooked or ignored in the current biomedical system. So maybe disabled people don't "suffer" from the disability they've been labeled with, but from their lack of privileges.[23] Then, there would be no need to dive into cyborgian fantasies. Instead of changing one's body with technology, wouldn't it be more fruitful to change the societal conditions that "disable" certain people in the first place?[24]

Perhaps the aforementioned idea of species-typical functioning is based on the ideology of non-disabled philosophers, who cannot conceive of living a disabled life as rewarding. Maybe we don't have to interfere with anyone's decisions at all. If people want to alter their bodies with technology—be it for "average" or "better than average" functionality—maybe they should be free to do so.[25]

If we follow the argument that "any body is possible," we lose sight of the meaning that the whole debate has for the conventionally disabled. Only specific abilities are considered important while others are deemed unimportant. Historically, such a discourse has led to discrimination against certain people who were categorized as lacking certain abilities. For example, the exclusion of women from higher education was justified, at least partly, through the judgment that women didn't have the requisite cognitive abilities. There are expectations about what abilities one must have to be fully included in society. Perhaps the way the enhancement enthusiasts instrumentalize people with disabilities just degrades those people.[26]

Would You Kindly Evolve Today?

So, is it morally permissible to use human enhancement technologies? In *BioShock* and *BioShock 2*, we can experience what it's like to survive in a society that has been ruined by an unregulated use of enhancement technologies. This apocalyptic presentation shows some of the most terrible consequences these technologies could have. Perhaps the *BioShock* games are a call for regulation, maybe even for a prohibition of these technologies. But the games are also a recognition of the possibilities. The debate needs to continue in the real world after the game is over.

Notes

1. Norman Daniels, "Normal Functioning and the Treatment–Enhancement Distinction," *Cambridge Quarterly of Healthcare Ethics* 9, no. 3 (2000): 309–322.
2. See Francis Fukuyama, *Our Post-Human Future: Consequences of the Biotechnology Revolution* (London: Profile Books, 2003).
3. See Nicholas Agar, "Whereto Transhumanism? The Literature Reaches a Critical Mass," *Hastings Center Report* 37, no. 3 (2007): 12–17.
4. See Anders Sandberg and Nick Bostrom, *Whole Brain Emulation: A Roadmap* (Oxford: Future of Humanity Institute, Oxford University, 2008).
5. See Martha J. Farah, Judy Illes, Robert Cook-Deegan, et al., "Neurocognitive Enhancement: What Can We Do and What Should We Do?" *Nature Reviews: Neuroscience* 5 (2004): 421–425; Anjan Chatterjee, "Brain Enhancements in Healthy Adults," in *Neuroethics in Practice: Medicine, Mind, and Society*, eds. Anjan Chatterjee and Martha J. Farah (New York: Oxford University Press, 2013), 3–15.
6. See Anders Sandberg, "Morphological Freedom—Why We Not Just Want It, but Need It," in *The Transhumanist Reader: Classical and Contemporary Essays on the Science, Technology, and Philosophy of the Human Future*, eds. Max More and Natasha Vita-More (Oxford: Wiley-Blackwell, 2013), 56–64.
7. Ibid.
8. See Andy Clark, *Natural-Born Cyborgs: Minds, Technologies, and the Future of Human Intelligence* (Oxford: Oxford University Press, 2003); James Hughes, *Citizen Cyborg: Why Democratic Societies Must Respond to the Redesigned Human of the Future* (Cambridge, MA: Westview Press, 2004); Kevin Warwick, *I, Cyborg* (Urbana, IL: University of Illinois Press, 2004).
9. See Nick Bostrom, "Why I Want to Be a Posthuman When I Grow Up," in *Medical Enhancement and Posthumanity*, eds. Bert Gordijn and Ruth Chadwick (Berlin: Springer, 2008), 107–137.
10. See Anjan Chatterjee, "Cosmetic Neurology: The Controversy over Enhancing Movement, Mentation, and Mood," *Neurology* 63, no. 6 (2004): 968–974.
11. See Fukuyama, *Our Posthuman Future*, 157; Michael J. Sandel, *The Case against Perfection: Ethics in the Age of Genetic Engineering* (Cambridge, MA: Harvard University Press, 2007).
12. See John Harris, *Enhancing Evolution: The Ethical Case for Making Better People* (Princeton, NJ: Princeton University Press, 2007).

13. Allen Buchanan, Dan W. Brock, Norman Daniels, and Daniel Wikler, *From Chance to Choice: Genetics and Justice* (Cambridge: Cambridge University Press, 2000).

14. See Veljko Dubljevic, "Toward a Legitimate Public Policy on Cognition-Enhancement Drugs," *AJOB Neuroscience* 3, no. 3 (2012): 29–33.

15. Ibid.

16. See Nikolas Rose, *The Politics of Life Itself: Biomedicine, Power, and Subjectivity in the Twenty-First Century* (Princeton, NJ: Princeton University Press, 2007).

17. See Melinda Cooper, *Life as Surplus: Biotechnology and Capitalism in the Neoliberal Era* (Seattle, WA: University of Washington Press, 2008); Bernard Lo and Marilyn J. Field, *Conflict of Interest in Medical Research, Education, and Practice* (Washington, DC: National Academic Press, 2009).

18. Jürgen Habermas, *The Future of Human Nature* (Cambridge: Polity, 2009).

19. See Muireann Quigley and John Harris, "To Fail to Enhance Is to Disable," in *Philosophical Reflections on Disability*, eds. D. Christopher Ralston and Justin Ho (London: Springer, 2010), 123–132; Julian Savulescu and Guy Kahane, "The Moral Obligation to Create Children with the Best Chance of the Best Life," *Bioethics* 23, no. 5 (2009): 274–290.

20. See Jackie Leach Scully and Christoph Rehmann-Sutter, "When Norms Normalize: The Case of Genetic Enhancement," *Human Gene Therapy* 12 (2001): 87–96.

21. See Alice Domurat Dreger, *One of Us: Conjoined Twins and the Future of Normal* (Cambridge, MA: Harvard University Press, 2004).

22. See Savulescu and Kahane, "The Moral Obligation."

23. See Bill Hughes, "Being Disabled: Towards a Critical Social Ontology for Disability Studies," *Disability & Society* 22, no. 7 (2007): 673–684; Fiona Kumari Campbell, *Contours of Ableism: The Production of Disability and Ableness* (Basingstoke: Palgrave Macmillan, 2008).

24. See Harlan D. Hahn and Todd L. Belt, "Disability Identity and Attitudes toward Cure in a Sample of Disabled Activists," *Journal of Health and Social Behavior* 45, Dec. (2004): 453–464.

25. See Anita Silvers, "A Fatal Attraction to Normalizing: Treating Disabilities as Deviations from 'Species-Typical' Functioning," in *Enhancing Human Traits: Ethical and Social Implications*, ed. Erik Parens (Washington, DC: Georgetown University Press, 1998), 95–123.

26. See Gregor Wolbring, "Ethical Theories and Discourses through an Ability Expectations and Ableism Lens: The Case of Enhancement and Global Regulation," *Asian Bioethics Review* 4, no. 4 (2012): 293–309.

Vending Machine Values
Buying Beauty and Morality in *BioShock*

Michael J. Muniz

Beauty may be beyond mere human understanding, whether or not we have ADAM. But what better way to help us understand beauty than our notorious plastic surgeon Dr. J.S. Steinman? Through a series of provocative recordings left throughout the Medical Pavilion, Steinman enlightens the player with his philosophy on beauty and morality. Beginning with his ever so humble approach to his own value system, Steinman says:

> I am beautiful, yes. Look at me, what could I do to make my features finer? With ADAM and my scalpel, I have been transformed. But is there not something better? What if now it is not my skill that fails me... but my imagination?

Steinman indicates that his ability to understand beauty is limited by his imagination. So, let us imagine instead, and see if we can understand it.

What Is Beauty?

Beauty, as it has been traditionally defined, is an ultimate value, an ideal on the same level as truth and goodness. These three values, according to Plato (*c.* 428–347 BCE), guide our rational desires. Plato writes in his *Symposium*:

BioShock and Philosophy: Irrational Game, Rational Book, First Edition. Edited by Luke Cuddy.
© 2015 John Wiley & Sons, Inc. Published 2015 by John Wiley & Sons, Inc.

> Beauty, then, is the destiny or goddess of parturition who presides at birth, and therefore, when approaching beauty, the conceiving power is propitious, and diffusive, and benign, and begets and bears fruit: at the sight of ugliness she frowns and contracts and has a sense of pain, and turns away, and shrivels up, and not without a pang refrains from conception.[1]

Beauty connects our attraction to truth and our desire for goodness. It might seem contradictory, or a bit off balance, but when you apply this connection, beauty is the completion to everything we know. Now I'm sounding a bit like Steinman.

Perhaps Steinman is on to something when he says the following in a recording found near the Surgery Foyer:

> Today I had lunch with the Goddess. "Steinman," she said… "I'm here to free you from the tyranny of the commonplace. I'm here to show you a new kind of beauty." I asked her, "What do you mean, Goddess?" "Symmetry, dear Steinman. It's time we did something about symmetry…"

Perhaps Steinman's "Goddess" is Plato's "goddess." And yet, Steinman's mention of the symmetrical is also an ancient property of beauty that Aristotle (*c.* 384–322 BCE) discusses. In fact, Aristotle says, "The chief forms of beauty are order and symmetry and definiteness."[2] Many of the ancient Greeks believed that symmetry represented order, and order was beautiful because it revealed a type of cosmic justice and truth that no person could deny. So, when Steinman's application of beauty comes into play, he is definitely emphasizing the order and justice that beauty provides.

We'll connect beauty and justice shortly, but for the moment let's consider how beauty and truth relate. The great romantic poet John Keats (1795–1821) wrote in his famous poem "Ode on a Grecian Urn":

> When old age shall this generation waste,
> Thou shalt remain, in midst of other woe
> Than ours, a friend to man, to whom thou say'st,
> "Beauty is truth, truth beauty, — that is all
> Ye know on earth, and all ye need to know."

This may be the very poem that provided Steinman the motivation to play with ADAM and perfect the appearance of age as much as he could. Perhaps the best evidence of his ADAM-based obsession and how his fascination with beauty has altered his view of the world—of truth—can be found in another recording of his near the Gatherer's Garden. He says:

> Not only are those little girls veritable ADAM factories, they're nearly indestructible. They regenerate any wounded flesh with stem versions of the dead cells. But their relationship with the implanted slugs is symbiotic... if you harvest the slug, the host will die. "So you see, it's not like killing," Tenenbaum said. "It's more like removing a terminal patient from life support."

Even though it may seem to be coming from Tenenbaum, it is actually Steinman's acceptance of this thought that fulfills his desire. So, truth and beauty do belong together. And, unfortunately for Steinman, his ideal form of beauty overpowered his judgment and his ability to perceive truth. Ultimately, this convolution of beauty and truth even interfered with symmetry, the only hope left for Steinman. Evidence of his attempt to reason his way out of symmetry can be heard in his own words, in his own voice (not recorded): "Why do we have two eyes? Is there some law that says we must? Two arms, two legs, two ears, two breasts..."

Steinman's Justice through Beauty

The player of *BioShock* is introduced to a world quite familiar to ours, not necessarily in the sense of Rapture, underwater cities, or vintage décor, but rather in the form of worldview. Does beauty somehow dictate what is right or wrong? Most people would instantly respond with a "no." But the connection actually goes back to Aristotle, who says, "beauty depends on magnitude and order."[3] Actually, the order Aristotle refers to in this quote is not the same as the order of justice, but people tend to mix them up.

I live in Miami, Florida (actually Hialeah, but that's not the point), and so-called beautiful people constantly surround me. Now, there is no spoken rule or doctrine that I know of regarding beauty and morality down here in Miami, but there seems to exist a silent understanding that you need to be beautiful in order to succeed. The fashion industry, beachfront tourism, and the plastic surgery market are the big moneymakers in Miami. So, when it comes to young people entering this world for the first time, beauty becomes a mandatory value that dictates their life. Usually, it's so obvious that even Dr. Steinman would be proud.

I think this concept applies beyond Miami. There seems to be a whole world of justice that is aligned with beauty. People are required to dress "appropriately" when interviewing for a job or attending a funeral. But style and taste have become so subjective that it is hard to determine a right or wrong sense of beauty. Steinman's blurring desire to make people beautiful would either drive him into further madness or make him the prime example of sanity if he walked along the boardwalk of South Beach. I can hear him now, just like he would say in the game when Jack enters the room:

> What can I do with this one, Aphrodite? She—won't—stay—still! I want to make them beautiful, but they always turn out wrong! That one, too fat! This one, too tall! This one, too symmetrical! And now... What's this, Goddess? An intruder?! He's ugly! Ugly! Ugly! UGLYYYYYYYY!

I sometimes ask my students to consider a disturbing scenario: Suppose a sick and twisted millionaire (someone like Fontaine) offered you $1 million if you threw a sack filled with six of the cutest and cuddliest puppies you've ever seen into a fire pit and you have to watch them burn to death before receiving the money. Would you do it? A large percentage of students say "no." Then, in a second scenario I ask those students who said "no" if it would make a difference if the bag had been filled with rats of the same size who would feel the same pain from the fire. Almost instantly, many respond "yes." When asked why, the most common answer is because rats are ugly. That's it! Simply put, because X is ugly, X should be tortured to death by fire, and I should be rewarded for watching it.

In his book *Art as Experience*, American philosopher and educator John Dewey (1859–1952) discusses the way children are easily manipulated and influenced by their perceptions of beauty and how it affects their development of moral judgments. Ultimately, Dewey suggests that the mindset of the young is such that whatever is beautiful and attractive should manage human behavior. My favorite *BioShock* villain would agree with the children:

> With genetic modifications, beauty is no longer a goal or even a virtue, it is a moral obligation. Do we force the healthy to live with the

contagious? Do we mix the criminal with the law-abiding? Then why are the plain allowed to mingle with the fair?!

Just think about every time you watch an episode of *COPS* on TV, or primetime local news, and see how criminals are often portrayed. They're never pretty, are they? Psychologists and sociologists have field days about how media depictions of criminals affect moral judgments, especially those based on race, gender, and ethnicity. So, therein lies the dilemma: Do we perceive something as beautiful because it is morally good, or do we perceive something as morally good because it is beautiful? Likewise, do we perceive something as ugly because it is morally wrong, or do we perceive something as morally wrong because it is ugly?

The Value of Beauty and Morality

There are two kinds of value. The first type of value in this circus of thought is intrinsic value. To have intrinsic value is for something to be important in and of itself. Happiness and love are examples of intrinsic values. Think, again, of a Little Sister and your decision to harvest or not to harvest her ADAM. If you decide to save her, it could mean that you believe she has intrinsic value and the amount of ADAM she yields is of little to no importance. However, if you decide to harvest a Little Sister it could mean that you believe she has only extrinsic value, the kind of value that can be attached to something or someone by something or someone else. The vending machines are not coincidentally called the Circus of Values. As players, we have value in surviving (intrinsic) so we'll do whatever we can to survive, including buying or hacking vending machines with supplies (extrinsic value). Now, to value beauty and morality as either intrinsic or extrinsic is a matter of choice. To choose one is to decide the fate of the other. Let me explain.

Gamers and game designers value *BioShock*. The "shock" is the reality of the mantra that fate is determined at birth. There are some philosophers, like Lady Gaga (who might succeed as a character in the *BioShock* universe), who preach the following platitude: biology is destiny (a.k.a. "I was born this way"). As a voice of reason, I most respectfully disagree. If I was born with a deformity that made me appear ugly to others, that does not mean that I am morally obligated to remain deformed for the rest of my life, and that I should never seek some sort of cure for my deformity. Please don't think of me as a type of Fontaine who has used his voice of reason to trick you into believing that ADAM is good, and that Steinman was mostly right when he says the following in an audio diary found on the desk in Emergency Access:

> Ryan and ADAM, ADAM and Ryan... all those years of study, and was I ever truly a surgeon before I met them? How we plinked away with our scalpels and toy morality. Yes, we could lop a boil here, and shave down a beak there, but... but could we really change anything? No. But ADAM gives us the means to do it. And Ryan frees us from the phony ethics that held us back. Change your look, change your sex, change your race. It's yours to change, nobody else's.

As the world of *BioShock* continues to grow, how else would I get your attention if not to shock you into using your Plasmid-reduced minds? Because I value choice, I choose to be who I am, not to conform to who I was supposed to be when I was born. So, values (like beauty and goodness) may be related somehow to what we believe. Like a level map in *BioShock*, my beliefs are an atlas (pun intended) to my reality. My beliefs are like the deep shaft beneath the Lighthouse from which my actions flow. One might even say—a philosopher certainly would—that believing in the things I do is the most important thing about me. Our understanding of values such as beauty and goodness can lead to either our success or our downfall. Just think of Steinman's portrait in *BioShock 2*, which depicts him as some sort of religious leader praising his failures in the form of a crucifixion.

This Is the End

Do beauty and morality depend on one another like a Little Sister depends on a Big Daddy? The *BioShock* series seems to answer "yes," depicting the ugly, distorted, and deformed as evil, and the beautiful and delicate as good. But just because we are players does not mean that we need to be played by such depictions. Ultimately, it is our choice and our responsibility to disentangle beauty and goodness and choose values for ourselves.

Notes

1. Plato, *Symposium and Phaedrus*, trans. Benjamin Jowett (New York: Dover Publications, 1993), 29.
2. Aristotle, *The Metaphysics*, trans. W.D. Ross, http://classics.mit.edu//Aristotle/metaphysics.html.
3. Aristotle, *Poetics*, trans. S.H. Butcher (New York: Dover Publications, 1997), 14.

Notes on Contributors

James Cook is a postgraduate student who dwells in a tiny Scottish town known mainly for its golf courses—a welcome respite from the political turmoil of Columbia. He researches philosophy of language, metaphysics, and some philosophy of philosophy, with the hopes of creating some kind of dissertation that features them all. When he isn't doing this he works various odd jobs, plays a bit of guitar, and drinks ale.

Luke Cuddy is an Assistant Professor of Philosophy at Southwestern College in Chula Vista, CA. He edited *The Legend of Zelda and Philosophy*, *World of Warcraft and Philosophy*, and *HALO and Philosophy*. An avid guitar player as well as gamer, he continues to annoy his friends with impromptu performances of "Will the Circle Be Unbroken."

Tyler DeHaven graduated from Ithaca College, NY, with a bachelor's degree. He finished with a major in philosophy, a minor in classical studies, and was also a member of Ithaca College's Honors Program. As an undergraduate, Tyler co-authored the "Halo as Apocalypse: Video Games and Revelatory Literature" chapter of *Halo and Philosophy: Intellect Evolved*. Though he hopes to attend law school one day, he admits that Rapture's "legal system" has a certain appeal…

BioShock and Philosophy: Irrational Game, Rational Book, First Edition. Edited by Luke Cuddy.
© 2015 John Wiley & Sons, Inc. Published 2015 by John Wiley & Sons, Inc.

Rick Elmore has a PhD in philosophy from DePaul University, Chicago, IL. He works primarily in the areas of contemporary French philosophy and critical theory, with a focus on issues of violence, ethics, and animal studies. Although an avid fan of the *BioShock* series, it remains for him an open question whether anyone really chooses or whether slaves ever truly obey. Rick is currently a visiting Faculty Fellow in Philosophy at Colby College, Waterville, ME.

Chris Hendrickson graduated from Ithaca College, NY, in 2010 with a bachelor's degree in planned studies: games and society. Chris co-authored the "Apocalypse as Halo" chapter in *Halo and Philosophy*, and his favorite game genres include fighting and adventure. He is currently working to become a professional singer in southern California, but if he knew where the lighthouse rocket was located he would join Columbia's Gayest Quartet in a heartbeat!

Charles Joshua Horn is an Assistant Professor of Philosophy at the University of Wisconsin, Stevens Point, WI. He finished his PhD work at the University of Kentucky and specializes in seventeenth- and eighteenth-century philosophy, with particular interests in Spinoza, Leibniz, and Kant. He contributed a chapter entitled "Dreams and Possible Worlds: *Inception* and the Metaphysics of Modality" to *Inception and Philosophy: Because It's Never Just a Dream*, published by Wiley-Blackwell, and also "The Triforce and the Doctrine of the Mean" in *The Legend of Zelda and Philosophy*, published by Open Court. Joshua has massive modal anxiety about what his counterparts might be doing in other possible worlds.

László Kajtár has a small hardware store in Rapture. Besides one unfortunate occasion of a Big Daddy smashing through the storefront, life is more or less fine. In his spare time, he likes to play a simulation game in which he's a doctoral candidate of philosophy at Central European University, Budapest, Hungary, and he's writing his thesis on the philosophy of storytelling.

Oliver Laas is a graduate student at the department of philosophy in the Estonian Institute of Humanities in Tallinn University, Estonia. His research interests include metaphysics, philosophy of language, philosophy of information, metaethics, information ethics, semiotics, and game studies.

Simon Ledder is a PhD student at the research training group "Bioethics" at the University of Tübingen, Germany. After majoring in sociology and media studies, he now deals with the construction of "human enhancement," "disability," and "normalcy" in contemporary media.

James McBain is an Associate Big Daddy of Philosophy at Pittsburg State University, KS. When he's not stalking the halls and classrooms protecting his Little Students, he can be found drilling into and, despite having a heavy drill for a hand, writing on epistemology, metaphilosophy, and ethics. Most carnage happens when people try to harvest in his course "Values and Video Games."

Rachel McKinnon is an Assistant Professor in the Department of Philosophy at the College of Charleston, SC. Her primary research focuses on the norms of assertion, and the relationship between knowledge and action. She has published on a variety of topics, including the norms of assertion, luck, weakness of will, and stereotype threat. Her recent work has appeared in *Metaphilosophy*, *Hypatia*, *Dialogue*, *Philosophical Psychology*, *Philosophical Studies*, and *American Philosophical Quarterly*. She fell in love with the original *BioShock*, and she's an avid gamer of both video and table-top games.

Robert M. Mentyka is currently a second-year PhD candidate at SUNY, Buffalo, NY, focusing on military ethics, bioethics, and continental thought. He completed his undergraduate degree at Franciscan University in Steubenville, OH, and considers himself an avid video gamer in his spare time. He honestly wouldn't mind working with a maniacal AI like SHODAN, but can't take the risk when so many papers are coming due.

Michael J. Muniz is currently a night-time Adjunct Professor at University of Phoenix, AZ, Northwood University, FL, and most recently at West Coast University, Irvine, CA, where he teaches medical ethics... a course Dr. Steinman would appreciate. He lives in sunny South Florida, with his aesthetically pleasing wife. He is trying to pursue a PhD in something, but colleges keep rejecting him due to his Ryan-esque personality. So, in the meantime, he teaches high school English and philosophy, trying to prevent the girls from becoming Little Sisters and the boys from becoming Big Daddies.

Catlyn Origitano is a PhD candidate in philosophy at Marquette University, Milwaukee, WI. Her main areas of research are ethics and aesthetics. Catlyn was also a contributor to the *Veronica Mars and Philosophy* series and she never rows!

Collin Pointon is a writer, teacher, and gamer in Seattle. He is definitely a slave to video games and philosophizing about them. Other than that, he completed a master's degree in philosophy at Marquette University, Milwaukee, WI, in 2013—miraculously without resorting to splicing. Recent works of his include the chapter "Lies Were More Dependable Than the Truth" in *Ender's Game and Philosophy*, published by Open Court, and "Can Video Games Find a Home in Aesthetics?," a presentation at the 2013 International Congress of Aesthetics. He encourages everyone, incessantly, to check out more of his work on his website.

Jason Rose is a PhD student in the Philosophy and Literature program at Purdue University, Lafayette, IN. His studies focus on ethics, aesthetics, and the philosophy of mind. A lifelong gamer, much of Jason's research involves games and the phenomenon of play, like his master's thesis "Emotion and Rhetoric in *Bioshock*." He is very pleased that playing *BioShock* 16 times actually ended up being useful research!

In our universe **Stefan Schevelier** studies social and political philosophy at the Radboud University of Nijmegen, the Netherlands. His research focuses on *cosmopolitanism*, or the idea that all human beings are part of the same moral community. Behind the doors of different lighthouses he fights Splicers for a living and writes philosophical papers for fun.

Scott Squires is a philosophy student at Pittsburg State University, KS. He is a graduate of Heartland Christian College in Newark, MO, and serves as a part of a pastoral leadership team at Covenant Harvest

Church in Pittsburg. While not looking to start a tyrannical cult through philosophy, theology, or any other "ology," in the spirit of taking the good and leaving out the bad, he would like to see Columbia's skylines installed all over the country to alleviate the parking problems on college campuses.

Roger Travis is an associate professor in the department of literatures, cultures, and languages at the University of Connecticut, Storrs, CT. He holds an AB from Harvard College and a PhD in comparative literature from the University of California, Berkeley. His research centers on links between ancient epic and digital games. He doesn't *think* anyone can control his actions with a simple phrase. Unless of course the phrase is "fries with that?"

Index

BioShock and Philosophy: Irrational Game, Rational Book, First Edition. Edited by Luke Cuddy.
© 2015 John Wiley & Sons, Inc. Published 2015 by John Wiley & Sons, Inc.